HOW TO BUILD RUSTIC FURNITURE

Smith Brook Press

Y0-ABC-106

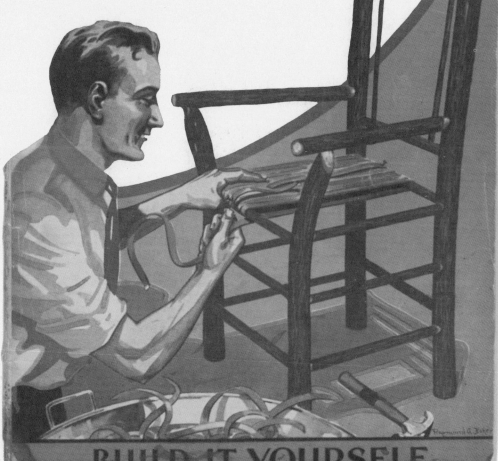

BUILD IT YOURSELF

HOW TO BUILD RUSTIC FURNITURE
Compiled By
Ed Smith

Published By
SMITH BROOK PRESS
Diamond Point Road
Diamond Point, NY 12824

All rights reserved. No part of this book may be reproduced or transmitted in any form or by any means, electronic or mechanical, including photocopying, recording or by any information storage or retrieval system without written permission from the author, except for the inclusion of brief quotations in a review.

Copyright © 1991 Edward W. Smith
Printed in the U.S.A.

ISBN 0-9629800-1-3

This planbook has been compiled from articles originally published during the early 1900's. Most of them have not been available since that time. We at Smith Brook Press are proud to bring them back in a series of planbooks that provide a wealth of ideas for our fellow craftspeople.

NOTE; Some of the methods and materials may now be outdated. We have reviewed every plan, however we cannot guarantee the safety or workability of any plan or suggested idea. Smith Brook Press and its owners disclaims any liability or responsibility for the use of this information or the actions of the purchaser. In other words use at your own risk, but most of all, please use common sense.

Sincerely,
Smith Brook Press

Dedicated To

Doris Blake
*without your help this book would
not have been possible.*

Acknowledgement

I would like to thank the following people for all their help.

Buck Larson and Jim Cranker - Technical Assistance
Dan Poynter and John Kremer - Inspiration
Martha, Billy, Jesse, Jamie and Kristie
for putting up with me.

EASY WAY TO BUILD *A Picturesque* RUSTIC SETTEE

BY A. C. SHUMAKER

RUSTIC settees of a type that will enhance any garden may be made at a cost of about 50 cents each by anyone who is willing to cut his own wood. I use willow, hickory, or sassafras found along streams, old fence rows, or in cut-over land. The hickory should be cut in the late fall or winter, otherwise it is likely to become wormy; but the other two can be cut at any time, and either worked up at once or allowed to dry. Only one kind of timber, and that all dry or all green, should be used.

The tools needed are a saw, an ax or heavy hatchet, a brace, one ⅞-in. auger bit, one ¼-in. bit, a claw hammer, and a yardstick. For a settee like that illustrated the following hardware is required:

1 lb. each of 4-, 6-, 8-, and 10-penny box nails; 1 lb. 16-penny spikes; 4 bolts, 3 by ¼ in.

To make the back, cut 1 top-rail *A* 1¾ to 2 in. in diameter (inside the bark) and 43 in. long; 1 bottom rail *B* the same diameter and 39 in. long; and 9 spindles *C* 1 to 1¼ in. in diameter and 13 in. long. For each end assembly, cut 1 back leg *E* 2½ to 3 in. in diameter and 34 in. long; 1 front leg *D* the same diameter and 24 in. long; 2 rungs *F* 1½ in. or more in diameter and 17 in. long; and 1 arm *G* 2 in. or more in diameter and 22 in. long. The following are also needed; 6 fairly straight lengths 1½ to 1¾ in. in diameter and 48 in. long for long rungs *H* and to cover ends of seat bottom as at *M*;

6 pc. about broom-handle size for braces *N*, *O*, etc; a number of straight lengths *L* ¾ to 1 in. in diameter for the seat bottom; and 2 pc. dressed lumber *K* 1 by 2½ by 48 in. for the seat supports.

THE best way to get what you want is to take saw, ax, and yardstick to the country. Notice how the arms and legs crook. The back legs and back rails crook to the back, the front legs to the side, and the arms also have a curve to the side. Knots and limbs do no harm; you can dress them down smooth.

Taper the ends of the rungs and top of the legs with an ax by placing the end on a solid block of wood. Don't cut them too small—just enough to start in a ⅞-in. hole. Make the back assembly as shown and lay it on the floor to see that all four ends of the rails touch.

Bore all holes (marked *J*) ⅞ in. in diameter and as deep as half the diameter of the wood. Drive the parts together, using a block of wood to protect the bark. Set the nail heads under the bark.

When the back and two end units are together, set the ends up, hang the back in place, and drive the back top-rail down to its position. This will give you the correct place to bore the holes for the bottom rail of the back. Lay the ends down and mark for the other long rungs—3 in. from the bottom of the legs for the bottom rungs and 15 in. up from the bottom for the rungs at the front and back of the seat. Put the back on the ends again and drive the parts solidly together, but don't nail. Spread the front so that it is about as long as the top of the back. You can then measure for your long rungs.

BE SURE the front and back legs touch the floor evenly and that the front looks to be in proper relation to the back. Drive all together and nail each rung.

Put on the braces as shown, then bolt on the dressed lumber for the seat supports, the top of which should be 15½ in. from the bottom of the legs. Cut small pieces the right length for the seat bottom and fasten with 4-penny box nails.

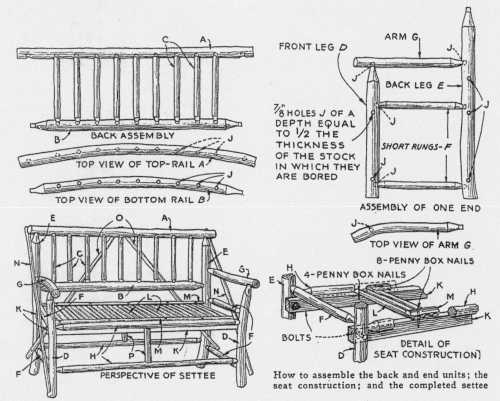

How to assemble the back and end units; the seat construction; and the completed settee

Split one of the long 1½ to 1¾ in. pieces, dress down smooth on the split side, and cut to fit over the ends of the seat bottom. Nail it through to the seat supports with 8-penny box nails.

Sandpaper lightly with No. 1½ sandpaper. If the wood is green, let the seat dry a few days; then apply a liberal coat of boiled linseed oil with a spoonful of red paint added to each pint of the oil.

LOG-CABIN BOOK ENDS
FOR RUSTIC SETTINGS

Split Branches Lend Realism to Walls of These Novelties

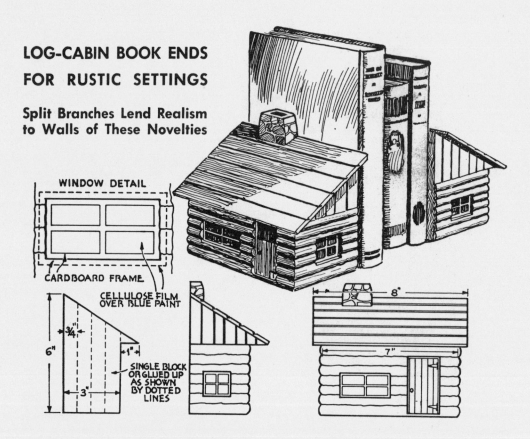

WINDOW DETAIL
CARDBOARD FRAME
CELLULOSE FILM OVER BLUE PAINT
¾"
6"
1"
3"
SINGLE BLOCK OR GLUED UP AS SHOWN BY DOTTED LINES
8"
7"

A BREATH of outdoors is brought to the den or study by these rustic book ends. Cut two blocks to the shape shown or glue them up from four thicknesses and a gable piece as indicated by the dotted lines. Make the roofs of thin strips of wood with the grooves cut at a slant; but make the cuts straight into the wood for the gabled ends.

Paint the window sections dark blue and cut cardboard frames for them, as illustrated. To create the illusion of glass, place cellulose film in each window area; then glue the frame over it. The edges of these frames will be covered when the logs—small, split branches—are nailed on. Groove the doors and glue on cardboard hinges. Insert big-headed pins cut short for knobs. A piece of sheet metal nailed to each cabin and extending under the books will prevent tipping. Glue felt on the underside.—GRAY WOLF.

Anyone with a lathe can build rustic-style pieces for cabin, home, porch, or lawn.

Furniture From the Forest

MOST rustic furniture has a shaggy, backwoods look that will win no beauty prizes. This set, which can be made without difficulty from small cedar logs, has light, clean lines that suit modern tastes. While a wood lathe will speed up the job, you could turn out the smaller pieces with hammer, saw, bit brace, and drawknife.

If you live in a town or city, materials can often be had by dickering with a farmer or landowner. Try to locate a dense second growth of cedar. From this you can probably cut sufficient dead material that's already fully seasoned. Select trees 1½" to 3" in diameter and cut them into convenient lengths. If there are no dead trees, cut green ones and dry thoroughly before use.

White cedar is the best material, spruce an excellent second choice. The grain of the latter may raise, however, unless the wood is very dry. For flat surfaces, such as chair arms, use red or yellow knotty pine. This blends well with either cedar or spruce when a natural finish is applied.

Begin with something relatively simple; for instance, a stool. This accomplished, make a bench, treating it as an elongated stool. From there, progress to a coffee table —simply a wider stool. By this time, you

will have acquired the feel of the work, and may choose from the entire field of rustic furniture. The variety of possible pieces is almost endless.

Let's see how a stool is made. From your stock select and cut one 2½" log 14" long, four 2¼" pieces 17½" long, two 2" pieces 12" long, and one 1¾" piece 13½" long. All diameters are of course approximate. In assembling vertical members place the smaller end at the top.

Put each piece in succession in a vise and peel with a drawknife. Remove only

Tenon joints secure most members, but where two pieces cross, carriage bolts should be used.

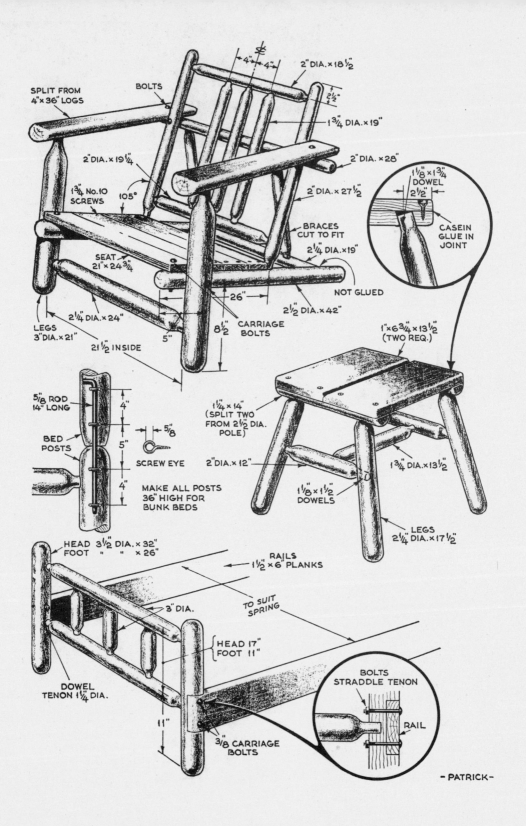

SPLIT FROM 4"× 36" LOGS

BOLTS

2" DIA. ×18½

2½ 4

1¾ DIA. ×19"

2" DIA. ×19¼

1¾ No.10 SCREWS

105°

2" DIA. ×28"

2" DIA. ×27½

1⅛ ×1¾ DOWEL 2½

CASEIN GLUE IN JOINT

BRACES CUT TO FIT

2¼ DIA. ×19"

NOT GLUED

SEAT 21"× 24¾

26"

2½ DIA. ×42"

CARRIAGE BOLTS

LEGS 3"DIA.×21"

2¼" DIA. ×24"

5"

8½"

21½ INSIDE

5/8 ROD 14" LONG

BED POSTS

4"

5"

4"

5/8 SCREW EYE

MAKE ALL POSTS 36" HIGH FOR BUNK BEDS

1"×6¾ ×13½ (TWO REQ.)

1"¼ ×14" (SPLIT TWO FROM 2½ DIA. POLE)

2"DIA. ×12"

1¾ DIA. ×13½

1⅛ ×1½ DOWELS

LEGS 2¼ DIA. ×17½

HEAD 3½" DIA. × 32" FOOT " " × 26"

RAILS 1½ ×6" PLANKS

3" DIA.

TO SUIT SPRING

HEAD 17" FOOT 11"

DOWEL TENON 1¼ DIA.

11"

3/8 CARRIAGE BOLTS

BOLTS STRADDLE TENON

RAIL

- PATRICK -

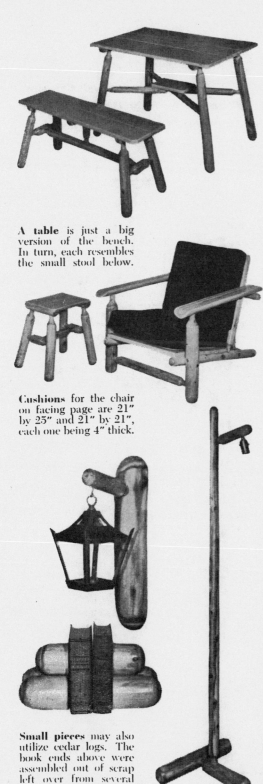

A **table** is just a big version of the bench. In turn, each resembles the small stool below.

Cushions for the chair on facing page are 21″ by 25″ and 21″ by 21″, each one being 4″ thick.

Small pieces may also utilize cedar logs. The book ends above were assembled out of scrap left over from several of the large projects.

the bark and a veneer of sap wood. Be careful to keep the blade from digging in. Cut off any large hard knots with a chisel and smooth with a small plane. This done, the poles are ready for the lathe.

Using a tailstock support, round off each end of the 14″ piece. I found this easiest with a very sharp 1″ flat chisel, ground to a slightly sharper angle than normally used for bench work. In fact, at no time during the building of this furniture was any other chisel used.

Treat the four 17¼″ pieces—the legs—in the same way, except that a dowel 1⅛″ in diameter is turned on the smaller end. Make each dowel about ½″ longer than the depth of the hole into which it is to be fitted. Turn similar dowels on each end of the three bracing pieces. Sand all the pieces smooth before removing from the lathe.

Now cut the two 1″ by 6¾″ by 13½″ seat boards to size. A slight chamfer on the abutting edges will improve the appearance of the finished article.

Saw or split the 14″ pole down the middle and smooth the flat faces. Attach under the seat boards with glue and 1¾″ flathead screws. When the glue has dried, trim off the protruding ends of the crosspieces. Also round the upper edges of the seat. Fill the countersunk screw holes with composition wood and sand smooth.

Drilling for the dowels is the trickiest job of all. Put the seat face down on the bench and mark centers for the leg-dowel holes. Set a bevel square at 8 deg. off the vertical, line the brace and bit so it is leaning outward at an angle of 98 deg. with the seat, and drill until the glue line is reached.

Drill the holes in the legs half way along their length, leaning the brace 8 deg. toward the dowel end. Drill the two side braces with the bit at 90 deg.

Put glue in the dowel holes and assemble the stool. When the glue is dry, check to make sure the legs are square on the floor. Three coats of clear lacquer, sanded lightly between coats, complete the job.

You're now ready for something more ambitious—a bench, table, chair, bed, or other item, chosen from the accompanying examples or designed on your own.

Arms for the chair and sofa are 4″ logs split down the middle. It's best to cut, peel, and rip these while they're still green, for small cracks often mar material of this size that's cut when dry.

LAWN FURNITURE

Take a tramp through the woods and gather up the stock needed to construct this distinctive set.

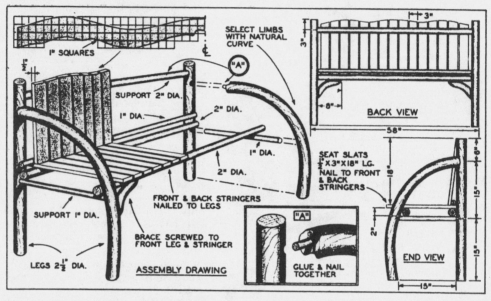

1" SQUARES

SELECT LIMBS WITH NATURAL CURVE

"A"

SUPPORT 2" DIA.

1" DIA.

2" DIA.

1" DIA.

2" DIA.

SUPPORT 1" DIA.

FRONT & BACK STRINGERS NAILED TO LEGS

BRACE SCREWED TO FRONT LEG & STRINGER

LEGS 2½" DIA.

ASSEMBLY DRAWING

3"

3"

BACK VIEW

8"

58"

SEAT SLATS ½"X3"X18" LG. NAIL TO FRONT & BACK STRINGERS

6"

18"

15"

2"

15"

END VIEW

15"

"A"

GLUE & NAIL TOGETHER

The two limbs for the front legs of the settee, which also serve as arm rests, should be selected with a natural curve. They should be long enough to join the back leg about 6 in. from the top, see photograph.

Y OUR front porch or yard will be a popular spot for outdoor gatherings, with this sturdy, attractive rustic furniture as the "bait." Cost of materials can be counted in pennies spent for nails and screws.

Lumber can be obtained by searching the woods in your vicinity for properly shaped limbs. Distinction is achieved by matching naturally twisted or bent limbs to form the arms and legs. Dead wood is all right if it's sound, or use green limbs seasoned in the sun for about two weeks. A coat of varnish will improve the appearance and help resist the weather.

You can vary the curve somewhat by holding the limb in a clamp during seasoning. For the front and back legs of the settee, fairly heavy limbs are desirable, about 2 in. in diameter. Supports and stringers can be made of

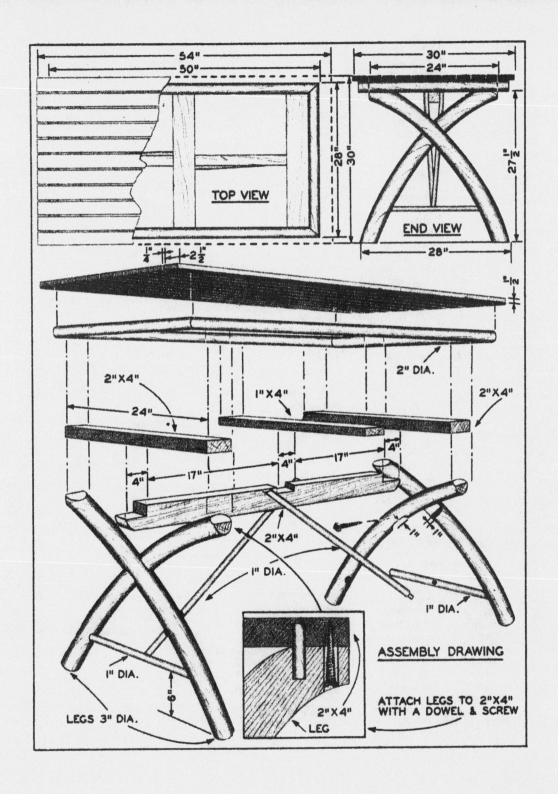

TOP VIEW

54"
50"

28"
30"

END VIEW

30"
24"

27 $\frac{1}{2}$"

28"

$\frac{1}{4}$"   2 $\frac{1}{2}$"

$\frac{1}{2}$"

2" DIA.

2"X4"

1"X4"

2"X4"

24"

17"   4"   4"   17"   4"

4"

2"X4"

1" DIA.

1" DIA.

1" DIA.

1" DIA.

1"   1"

6"

LEGS 3" DIA.

ASSEMBLY DRAWING

2"X4"

LEG

ATTACH LEGS TO 2"X4"
WITH A DOWEL & SCREW

smaller limbs. The easiest tool to use in removing the bark and leveling the knots is a spokeshave, though the bark will strip off easily if you can cut the limbs when the sap is running.

The first step in making the settee is to join the front to the back leg. Shape the end as shown in "A." Glue and secure by driving a nail through both members.

When both end sections have been asembled, drill the holes for the upper support in both back legs, approximately 3 in. from the top. Fit the upper support and nail the front and back stringers into place. The two braces, cut from twisted limbs and screwed to the front legs and stringer will add strength and rustic charm. Plane the top surfaces of the stringers level, and nail some boards to the stringers, spaced about ½ in. apart to allow for expansion and drainage. Plane the irregularities from the front face of the upper stringer and upper support and nail the back slats into place. Make certain that the boards are long enough to allow for the curve. The settee will easily accomodate three adults.

The frame of the table is similarly built from tree limbs. Miter the ends of the side and endpieces and assemble with screws to the 2x4 cross-members. Nail the center rib to the bottom side of the cross-members, and install the 1x4 cross-member by nailing to the center rib and through the two side-pieces.

The two legs for each end are joined together with a cross-bar and ⅜ in. lag screws before attaching to the frame. The detail for one of the legs, made of a sturdy 3 in. limb, is shown in the inset. Attach to the 2x4 cross-member with a dowel and screw for each leg. Plane the top level and nail the boards in place, and you'll have a thoroughly solid table with ample space for your guests.

While it is not absolutely necessary to take this furniture in during the winter, still and all, if there is no possibility of it being used during the winter months, you may as well bring it indoors in order to extend its life. Actually, with a bit of care, the life of the rustic lawn furniture should be equal to any piece of furniture you may have in your home.—*Edward R. Lucas*.

Swing Made of Hickory Sapling

A swing, so durable that it has become a virtual landmark, was made from a long, straight hickory sapling suspended from the limb of a tree. The sapling was split part of its length, as shown in the illustration, and a bolt put through it to prevent the upper portion from cracking. The lower end was smoothed off, so as not to injure the hands, and mortised through a slab of wood, as shown in the detailed sketch. A safe hook from which to suspend the swing is suggested. It is made from a bolt fixed through the limb and curled at the hook end  so that the swing may be taken down in bad weather.—Hubert Kann, Pittsburgh, Pa.

Left: Finished table ready for refreshments or a card game. Sections of top are glued up from shakes or regular lumber.

Lower left: A set of chairs like this are handy indoors or out. The original furniture was made of Western red cedar.

HERE'S something different for that shady spot in the backyard or the empty space at the end of the porch. It's a set of sturdy, lightweight furniture that's easy on the eye and the chassis when you relax in it. Best of all, the cost is almost nil for it's made of naturally bent tree limbs from the nearest woods, plus a handful of screws and nails.

When you're out hunting for the wood (preferably a soft one), choose limbs with a natural "elbow" or crook for the front legs and arms of the chair while for the back legs and rungs, pieces with a slight bow will do the trick. Start operations by gluing together the two side sections, consisting of the front and back legs, plus the side support. Then drill matching holes for the back rungs and supports (both front and back) allowing for an angle in drilling as the chair is 4 in. wider at the front than the back. After they are assembled and glued, level the tops of the upper front and back supports and nail the seat slats in place. Cut out the ends of the outer ones to clear the legs. The back slats are then nailed to their supports and the tops cut to the desired shape. Give the front of the seat slats the same treatment and follow it up by nailing the side pieces in place.

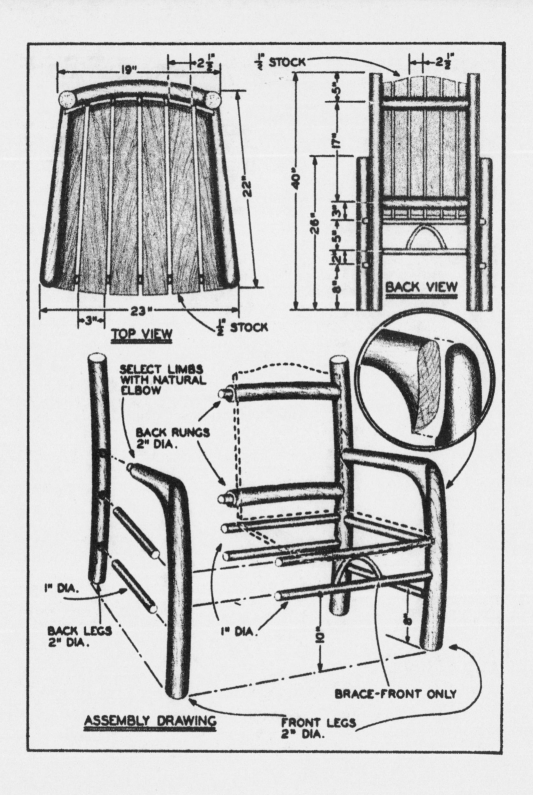

19"
2½"
22"
23"
3"
½" STOCK

TOP VIEW

½" STOCK
2½"
5"
17"
40"
26"
3"
5"
2"
8"

BACK VIEW

SELECT LIMBS
WITH NATURAL
ELBOW

BACK RUNGS
2" DIA.

1" DIA.

BACK LEGS
2" DIA.

1" DIA.

10"

6"

BRACE-FRONT ONLY

FRONT LEGS
2" DIA.

ASSEMBLY DRAWING

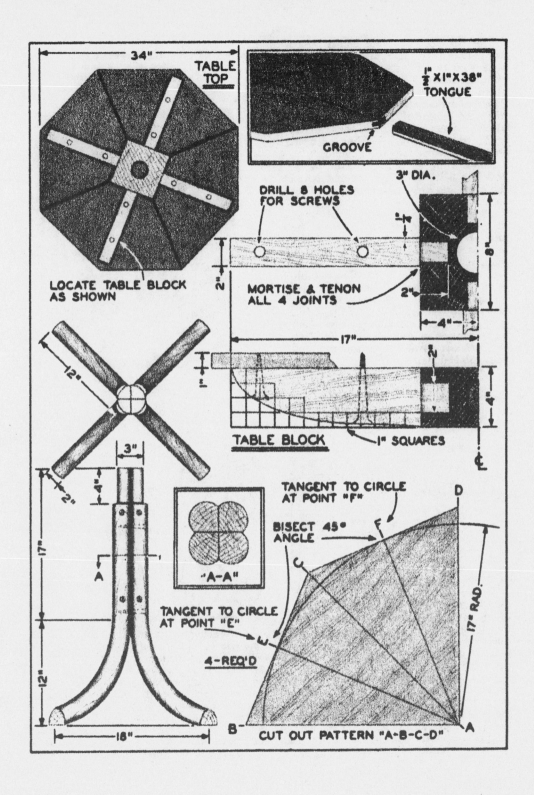

TABLE TOP

34"

$\frac{1}{2}$"X1"X38" TONGUE

GROOVE

LOCATE TABLE BLOCK AS SHOWN

DRILL 8 HOLES FOR SCREWS

3" DIA.

MORTISE & TENON ALL 4 JOINTS

2"

2"

8"

4"

17"

TABLE BLOCK

1" SQUARES

12"

3"

4"

2"

17"

12"

18"

A

"A-A"

4-REQ'D

TANGENT TO CIRCLE AT POINT "F"

BISECT 45° ANGLE

TANGENT TO CIRCLE AT POINT "E"

CUT OUT PATTERN "A-B-C-D"

17" RAD.

D

F

C

E

B

A

The base of the table comes next, using four naturally curved limbs cut square on two sides to form a roughly circular section. After the legs are glued and screwed together, cut them down to a diameter of 3 in. at the top to fit the hole in the table block. This piece is your next chore and can be made of commercial lumber or split from a deadwood log (if it's sound) with a shake knife as shown. Either way, bore the 3 in. hole, mortise and tenon the arms and dress their upper surfaces so they're level. Following this, drill the eight holes and glue the block in place over the 3 in. end of the base. The next step is to make a pattern for the four parts of the top and after cutting them to shape, rout out a ½ by ½ in. groove in the inside edges. To assemble the top, cut the two tongues and mortise for the intersection at the center. Then join all four sections on top of the block, leaving a narrow crack between them for expansion in wet weather. Apply a coat of clear varnish after sanding, and your job is done.

Below: Splitting boards from a log with the help of a shake knife. Deadwood can be used but it must be sound and dry.

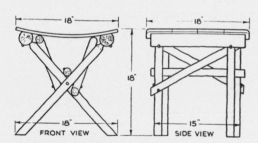

FRONT VIEW • SIDE VIEW

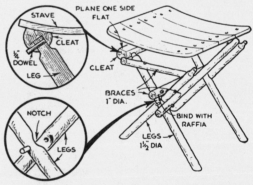

STAVE • PLANE ONE SIDE FLAT • CLEAT • ¼ DOWEL • LEG • CLEAT • BRACES 1" DIA. • BIND WITH RAFFIA • NOTCH • LEGS • LEGS 1½ DIA

OUTDOOR FURNITURE constructed of rough materials always harmonizes well with the natural setting of a garden or lawn. This stool made of saplings has a curved seat of old barrel staves. Trim, fit, and dress the staves as shown in the drawing, being sure to smooth any splintery edges. Countersunk screws hold the seat to two cleats made of saplings planed smooth on their top sides. The cleats are bored to take the shaped ends of the legs, and ¼″ dowels through the cleats into the ends of the legs secure the joints.

All bracing joints are also doweled, with one end of the dowels protruding as pegs. Where braces and legs cross, they are slightly notched to make for sturdiness. Binding the end joints of the straight brace with raffia will add strength and a touch of rustic craftsmanship.

The stool has no finishing of any kind, in keeping with its character. If desired, a set of these can be made for barbecue parties or back-yard picnics.—HI SIBLEY.

Rustic Picnic Table and Benches

By NORBERT ENGELS

MATERIALS for this rustic picnic table and benches are readily obtainable in most communities without any priorities. The cost—including two coats of the best waterproof varnish—should not greatly exceed $5, especially if one can cut his own materials.

Straight cedar fence posts 7' or 8' long should be selected. After cutting a suitable number the proper length for the table and bench tops, they must be ripped into halves. Use 4″ posts for the table top and 3″ posts for the benches. All cross bars are made from 3″ stock, but the table legs are made from 4″ stock.

If the posts are sawed on a bench power saw, one edge should first be slightly flattened or jointed to run along the ripping fence. This flat plane also serves as an excellent guide in sawing the table legs at parallel 60° angles. If

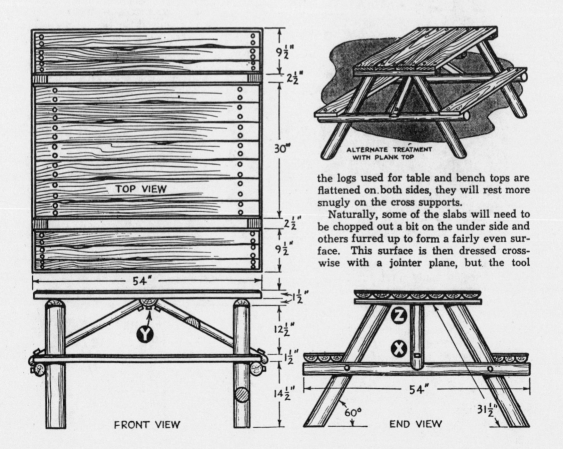

ALTERNATE TREATMENT WITH PLANK TOP

TOP VIEW

FRONT VIEW

END VIEW

the logs used for table and bench tops are flattened on both sides, they will rest more snugly on the cross supports.

Naturally, some of the slabs will need to be chopped out a bit on the under side and others furred up to form a fairly even surface. This surface is then dressed crosswise with a jointer plane, but the tool

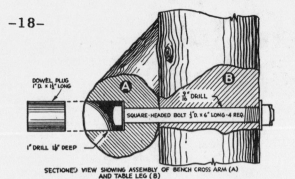

DOWEL PLUG
1" D. X 1½ LONG

9/16 DRILL

SQUARE-HEADED BOLT ½ D. X 6" LONG-4 REQ.

1" DRILL 1½ DEEP

SECTIONED VIEW SHOWING ASSEMBLY OF BENCH CROSS ARM (A)
AND TABLE LEG (B)

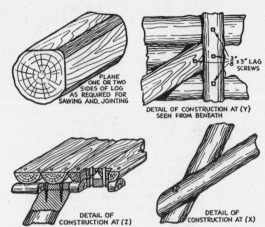

PLANE
ONE OR TWO
SIDES OF LOG
AS REQUIRED FOR
SAWING AND JOINTING

3/8 X 3" LAG
SCREWS

DETAIL OF CONSTRUCTION AT (Y)
SEEN FROM BENEATH

DETAIL OF
CONSTRUCTION AT (Z)

DETAIL OF
CONSTRUCTION AT (X)

marks are allowed to remain. The slabs are fastened with ⅜" dowels driven clear through in drilled holes, as shown.

An alternate plan is given for those who prefer to use planks for the table top and benches. In either case, the underpinnings are the same and the dimensions are identical.

CONSTRUCTING RUSTIC SWING SUPPORT

and four pieces 36 in. in length are required for the braces. The side rails are 5 ft. 6 in. long. The braces and side rails are smaller in diameter and are cut from the tops of the legs and top rail. Poles about 4 in. across at the bottom are the proper size to cut for this purpose and should be as nearly alike in size as possible. Bolts ½ in. in diameter are used at the top where the legs cross, and ¼-in. bolts serve for attaching the braces and side rails. This support can be taken down without difficulty in a short time and stored inside for the winter season.—HAROLD JACKSON.

SMALL logs or poles may be used in many ways for constructing rustic fixtures and furniture for the lawn and garden. The poles may be obtained in almost any woodland, along streams or rivers, and, if permission is asked, usually can be had for the cutting.

The support illustrated was made for an ordinary porch swing. Five logs 8 ft. 6 in. long are needed for the legs and top rail,

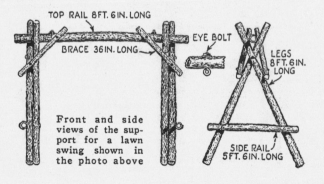

TOP RAIL 8FT. 6IN. LONG

BRACE 36IN. LONG

EYE BOLT

LEGS
8FT. 6IN.
LONG

Front and side views of the support for a lawn swing shown in the photo above

SIDE RAIL
5FT. 6IN. LONG

RUSTIC FURNITURE

WELL designed rustic furniture for open porches, lawns, gardens, and the summer cottage may well serve two admirable functions; improve the appearance of the locale, and provide comfort.

Rustic furniture, built of the right materials to serve definite needs,—has individuality. It is practically impervious to dents and scratches, and requires no varnish to give it a "finished" look. It is as harmonious in the summer home as the woods and waters that surround it, and as much in keeping with garden and lawn as the flowers and shrubs that give it the background. It is essentially a life-time furniture, withstanding all climatic conditions, remaining in the open thru storm and sunshine.

Perhaps second growth hickory is the best material of which to build the framework for rustic furniture. It is a

Nothing will add so much to the attractiveness of your lawn or garden as well designed rustic furniture. It is inviting to your friends and guests, and will render service for years.

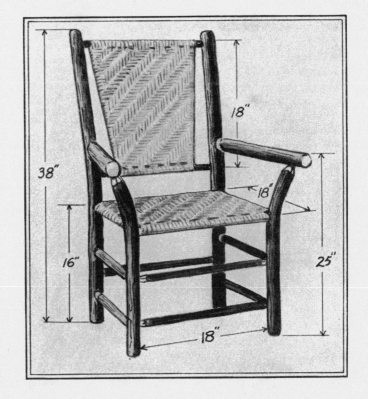

wood which is not only attractive in outdoor settings but it withstands the various onsloughts of the elements, and will last for a decade in the more rigorous climates. Certain manufacturers sell parts "knocked down," ready for assembly, and have a great variety of designs from which to select. However, the ambitious worker may get a real "kick" out of gathering his material from "nature in the raw," if he resides in a section of the country where second growth hickory grows. It will require labor, but the real craftsman never hesitates to spend time on construction if the end results are satisfactory.

Second growth hickory should be cut in the late fall for when cut at this season the bark will adhere firmly to the wood structure after it has seasoned. If one has decided upon the pieces he is to construct, he may select natural growth curves of branches to fit the curves of say, the arms or the front posts of a chair as illustrated at Fig. 1. Small branches should be cut fairly close to the main trunk, using care not to mar the bark.

Store the hickory in a dry place until it is well seasoned or, if possible, let some concern place it in a kiln to go through the usual process of drying.

Curved pieces may be given their form by steaming and then placing them in a form until essentially dry. This is not difficult to do, for hickory bends very easily without shearing or cracking.

When the wood is thoroughly seasoned the stub ends of branches are trimmed close to the bark and sanded smooth. The various parts are then carefully selected to match in texture and diameter and curves. Slight

An interesting group of rustic furniture for porch or lawn

Fig. 2

variations will not affect the general appearance of the piece of furniture.

While the most popular wood for rustic furniture is second growth, smooth bark hickory, the craftsman need not confine himself to this wood alone. He may use other woods such as tamarack, sassafras and rock elm, altho these will actually not stand up as well under varying weather conditions as the hickory.

Joints to Use

On such pieces as chairs, settees and tables, mortise and tenon joints should be used. Tenons on the curved pieces, such as the parts of the chair shown at Fig. 1, may be cut with a draw knife, and finished with any convenient cutting tool. Those on the straight pieces may be turned out on a lathe, or cut as just described, in the absence of a lathe. Be exceedingly careful to cut a tenon which runs parallel to the mortise an adequate distance, or the joint will not hold securely.

Bore the mortises with an auger bit. When ready to assemble a piece, make the joints a driving fit. Use a good grade of glue. To give additional security reinforce each joint with a galvanized nail. Fig. 1 shows a chair with woven seat and back. The essential dimensions for a comfortable chair are given, but it is, of course, necessary for the craftsman to fit dimensions to his own particular job. For instance, in the case of a rocker, he would need to cut the height from seat to ground; for a settee, he might double the width; for children, all dimensions would need to be altered.

Even tho the several pieces illustrated are rustic, this does not mean that chairs must be uncomfortable. These may, and do, afford unusual comfort, particularly where the seat and back are woven with a pliable material.

Materials which may be used are ash, or Indian splints, rattan, and inner hickory bark. These all stand up well under constant use and withstand weathering. But of the three, the inner bark is perhaps the best to use. It is cut from the inner bark of the hickory tree, and is exceedingly pliable when wet, making it a fine weaving medium. It is procurable in coils with strands varying in length from four to twelve feet. These strands are uniformly ¾″ wide.

Before weaving, the strands are soaked in water until they become thoroly pliable. They should not be kept in water too long or they are apt to discolor. Ordinarily one does not complete the weaving of a seat or back at one sitting. The worker may leave his work at any stage, but upon resuming operation he will need to soak the woven area thoroly. A sponge is excellent for the purpose.

How To Weave

A very comfortable, well designed chair is shown at Fig. 2. The dimensions for this are essentially the same as that at Fig. 1. After assembly, the weaving of the seat may be started. The cover of this issue shows grapphically how the operator works in wrapping the rails. A sketch showing the scheme of weaving is shown at Fig. 3. This is known as the diagonal weave, and is the one very generally followed for the simple reason that it is the easiest to do, and is, in addition, very effective.

Let us assume that everything is in readiness for weaving. Begin by tacking a strand, say, the front rail next to the post. Carry it over this rail and across to the back rail, then underneath to the starting rail. Continue to "wrap" the strand around the two rails in this fashion to the end of the strand. Tack the strand to the rail, wherever it runs out, as a temporary measure. Start a second strand, overlapping the other one about six inches, and continue warpping until it runs out. Repeat this process until the frame is fully wrapped. See that the strands are kept very close together, for there is shrinkage in drying.

Now refer to Fig. 4. This shows how the actual weaving is done in

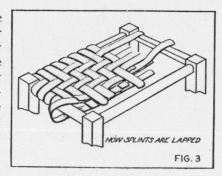

HOW SPLINTS ARE LAPPED

FIG. 3

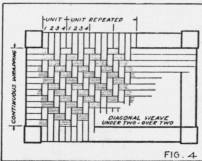

UNIT — UNIT REPEATED
1 2 3 4 — 1 2 3 4

CONTINUOUS WRAPPING

DIAGONAL WEAVE
UNDER TWO - OVER TWO

FIG. 4

"units." That is, this particular pattern is woven in four unrepeated strands. The units are then repeated until the tire area is woven. Begin, say, at a side rail near a post and weave exactly as the sketch shows, starting *under* two strands. The next time around, begin *over* one strand; the next time *over* two; and the last time *under* one. The balance of the weave is *under* two and *over* two. End each time at the rail just where the weaver leads. In other words, it is not possible to run under and over two in completing a weave at the rail. This process is repeated in units for the entire seat.

If the front rail is longer than the back, there will be a little space left next to the posts, which is filled in after the seat is woven. In such case, it is better to wrap the side rails first.

As the work proceeds, the ends are woven in which were overlapped in the wrapping, and new strands are added as illustrated at Fig. 3. The temporary tacks may be withdrawn as the ends are now held in place by the weaver.

The bottom of the seat should also be woven idenitcally to the top. Inasmuch as the diagonal weave is the simplest, use it regardless of the kind of pattern used above, or on the front of the back. Two of the more intricate designs will be discussed later.

Working Other Patterns

The craftsman who wishes to try a design a little more complicated than the diagonal pattern just described, may weave the back of his chair according to the pattern or design shown at Fig. 5. This is known as the diamond pattern inasmuch as the effect is that of a series of dia-

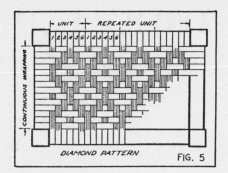

DIAMOND PATTERN   FIG. 5

For those who may at some time use ash splints or rattan for furniture, the suggestion is made that very effective designs may be worked out with the weavers of different widths and with two colors, or both.

A radial pattern or design is shown at Fig. 6. The weaving for this begins at the center, and is, therefore, manifestly more difficult than the two described, altho once begun, it requires only close attention to work. To begin this weave it is necessary to count the strands to locate the center one. The weaver runs over *three* at the center, then over two and under two in both directions. The second strand runs under one at the center, then over two and under two at the rails in both directions. The third strand runs under three at the center, then over two and under two in both directions. The fourth strand runs over one at the center, then over two and under two. This completes the unit. The sketch shows the method clearly. This design is very effective, but it should not be undertaken unless the area to weave is practically rectangular and reasonably large.

mond-shaped patterns over the entire area.

Weaving is begun just as described for the diagonal weaves, but the unit in this case is made up of six unrepeated weavers instead of four.

The unit of the Pattern at Fig. 5 is as follows:

Over 1, under 2, over 3, under 2, over 1.

Under 2, over 2, under 1, over 2, under 3.

Under 1, over 2, under 3, over 2, under 1.

Over 2, under 2, over 1, under 2, over 3.

Under 1, over 2, under 3, over 2, under 1.

Under 2, over 2, under 1, over 2, under 3.

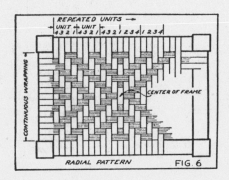

RADIAL PATTERN   FIG. 6

Make Many Pieces

The craftsman need not confine himself to the construction of chairs alone. He may make foot stools, tables, magazine holders, waste baskets, and other pieces, utilizing inner bark to embellish the pieces, even tho it serves no other purpose.

The sketches illustrate a few pieces which may be constructed. These will serve for years, and will add a distinct note to garden, lawn or porch, and provide comfort for summer days.

Comfortable Rustic Chair

MADE OF WILLOW BRANCHES

By

Elisabeth Frost Miner

BEAUTY, comfort, and outdoor durability distinguish the design of this rustic chair. The back and arms are supple willow reeds; the seat is made of flat-sided branches. For twenty years Joe Pak, of Riner, Va., has used a garden chair of this type—a demonstration of its durability.

Branches pruned from willow trees and saplings will furnish the material (see list at end of article). It is advisable to peel them.

Framework. Nail three 14-in. crossbars to back legs, spaced from bottom 6, 14, and 23 in. Join front legs with one 14-in. crossbar 6 in. from bottom, and another at least 24½ in. long across top ends, extending equally on each side. Nail C and D (about 6 in. long) between the front crossbars as shown.

Connect front and back leg frames with two 14-in. long crossbars on each side, spaced like front crossbars. Brace framework with six 17-in. long pieces as indicated in the bracing diagram. Fasten a 24½-in. cross bar marked A across and in back of the front legs about 3½ in. above B, and also nail it to C and D. Nail split logs on to form seat.

Arms. Soak willow for about twenty-four hours. Nail to side of back legs in succession,

Not only is this chair unusually graceful, but back and arms are somewhat springy

beginning at upper back crossbar. Nail other ends to A. Also nail each strip to the preceding one at intervals, and alternate spacing of nails in adjoining strips.

Back. Nail the well-soaked strips for the fan-shaped back filling to crossbars E and F. Nail the first of the 66-in. reeds G at extreme back of seat (at side, of course). Spread the back filling pieces to form a fan and nail through the first 66-in. reed into their ends as indicated. Then follow with the other four reeds. Use enough nails to secure well, but not so many that the wood is split.

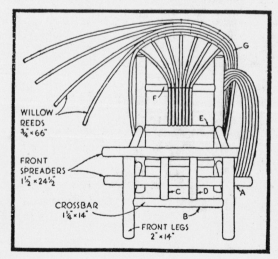

WILLOW REEDS ¾"×66"

FRONT SPREADERS 1½"×24½"

CROSSBAR 1¼"×14"

FRONT LEGS 2"×14"

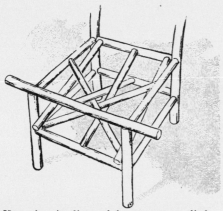

How the six diagonal braces are applied (some parts of the frame being omitted for clearness) and, at right, the general plan

No. Pc.	Dia.	Length	For
2	2	14	Front legs
2	2	28	Back legs
10	1⅝	16½	Split pieces for seat
2	1½	24½	Front spreaders (leave these longer and cut after assembly)
6	1½	17	Diagonal bracing
8	1¼	14	Crossbars
2	1¼	6	Front uprights
5	¾	42	Arms
7	¾	18	Fan-shaped back filling
5	¾	66	Back

List of Willow Branches

NOTE: Diameter and length are given in inches.

A Springy Hammock Support Made of Boughs

In many camping places, balsam branches, or moss, are available for

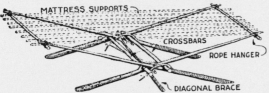

The Camp Bed can be "Knocked Down," or Transported Considerable Distances as It Stands

improvising mattresses. Used in connection with a hammock, or a bed made on the spot, such a mattress substitute provides a comfort that adds to the joys of camping. A camp hammock, or bed of this kind, is shown.

To make it, cut four 6-ft. poles, of nearly the same weight and 1 in. in diameter at the small end. These saplings should have a fork about 2½ ft. from the lower ends, as resting places for the crossbars, as shown. Then cut two poles, 2 in. in diameter and 3½ ft. long, and two smaller poles, 3 ft. long. Also cut two forked poles, 4½ ft. long, for the diagonal braces. Place two of the long poles crossing

each other, as shown, 1 ft. from the ground. Set up the second pair similarly. Fix the crossbars into place, in the crotches, the ends of the crotch branches being fastened under the op-

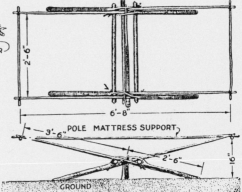

The Poles are Selected Carefully and Set Up with Stout Cross Braces at the Middle and Lighter Ones for the Mattress Support

posite crossbar. The end bars are fixed to the crossed poles by means of short rope loops. The mattress is placed on springy poles, 7 ft. long and 2 in. apart, alternating thick and thin ends. The moss is laid over the poles, and the balsam branches spread on thickly. Blankets may be used as a cover.—J. S. Zerbe, Coytesville, N. J.

Making Rustic Willow Furniture

THE lawn chair and settee shown here is made of material just as nature furnishes it. This furniture can be used on the porch as well as on the lawn or in the garden and is just the thing for the summer camp or cottage. It is made of willows that can be cut along any water course or ditch of any country road.

Willow Easily Worked

Willows are especially adapted to this kind of work for they grow straight with only a few small branches. They are also real springy which allows them to be bent into almost any desired shape. The legs or posts should be about one and one half inches across. All other parts should be three quarters of an inch to one inch in diameter. The seat may be made of sticks laid close together or of three quarter inch boards. The boards are generally the most satisfactory for the seat. The photograph shows a chair and a settee while the sketch shows only the settee. The chair is made identically except that it is half as long as the settee. The method of construction is exactly the same.

The measurements shown are approximately correct but in this kind of work where nothing is exactly straight the measurements will vary

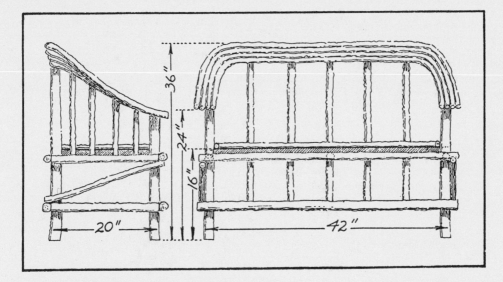

somewhat and some parts will have to be fitted to the places they are to occupy. However, the sketch gives a rough idea of how long to cut the parts. The boards used in making the seat are laid on cross runners between the corner posts at the ends. There is also one center support in the settee. The cross pieces are indicated by the dotted circles in the front view.

How to Assemble

The parts are assembled with wire nails, preferably galvanized. Several sizes will be needed for the different parts. The band at the back is made of four sticks. This is the last part put on and one stick is nailed on at a time and one on top of another until they are all in place. The finished furniture may be painted or just varnished in the natural which gives it a very rustic appearance.

This homemade willow furniture will give good service for a score of summers if it is stored in a fairly dry place during the winter months.

Rustic Flower Vases

A simple and effective flower container for the summer cottage or porch is made from a short length of a tree branch. The

bark gives a rustic appearance to the vase, and a variety of effects are obtainable by judicious selection, the white bark of the birch being the most conspicuous. The container may be made of any diameter by using a section of the desired size, from which the interior has been gouged or drilled out. A "liner," which is what florists call a container for water in such vases, may be provided by inserting a can, or other receptacle, into the hollow center.

Weave this OLD CHIHUAHUA Chair

by HI SIBLEY

FROM old Chihuahua province, on the southern banks of the Rio Grande, comes this artistic as well as comfortable chair for your lawn, porch, or sun room.

Not a single nail or screw is used in the entire chair—these were unheard of in the days when some Mexican, or possibly an Indian, first worked out the simple design. Rawhide lacings hold the frame together, and form the springy covering for the seat.

Select and gather your frame pieces first. For the vertical posts almost any American woods such as birch, oak, or ash saplings may be used once they are well seasoned. Hoops may be bent from ash or hickory slats by steaming or soaking in water. In weaving the rawhide for the chair seat, use the same care as you would in restring-

Front and back views of a completed Chihuahua chair as built by the Mexicans.

FISHLINE AND GLUE

SOFT LEATHER BINDING FOR ARMS AND BACK

CHAIR FRAME

SOFT LEATHER SEAT

SEAT HOOP

RAWHIDE LACINGS

LATTICE SPLINTS ARE 19" LONG

NOTCHES CUT ON DIAGONAL

2"

LOCATION OF THE UPRIGHTS

SEAT ASSEMBLY

BINDING

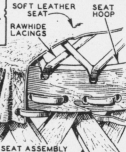

RAWHIDE LACING

SPLIT BAMBOO OR REED IN HERRING-BONE WEAVE

7"

SEAT PLAN

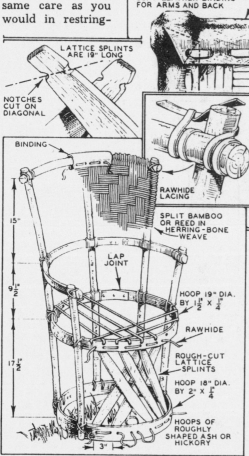

15"

9½"

17½"

LAP JOINT

HOOP 19" DIA. BY 1½" x ¼"

RAWHIDE

ROUGH-CUT LATTICE SPLINTS

HOOP 18" DIA. BY 2" x ¼"

HOOPS OF ROUGHLY SHAPED ASH OR HICKORY

3"

Fasten frame of chair together with leather thongs which have been soaking for several hours. Leather will shrink in drying, and hold pieces rigidly together. Use dry thongs for chair seat.

Cover seat of chair with soft leather, fastening to sides of seat hoop with leather thongs. Fasten each reed with fishline and glue in manner shown above, then cover with soft leather binding. Weaving is carried around to each side.

ing a tennis racquet, to maintain a circular shape yet have every string tight.

Rough slats or splints are notched and fastened at an angle around the bottom of the chair to give rigidity and an artistic effect at the same time. The split bamboo or reed used for the herring-bone weave at the back of the chair is now cut to the correct lengths for horizontal and vertical pieces. These thin reeds are held in place at each end with fishline and glue, and the ends later covered with a soft leather binding.

A coat of clear lacquer will preserve your chair against ravages of time and weather, yet leave the wood and reed in its natural color. Do not lacquer the leather. An occasional oiling or rubbing with lard will be sufficient to keep the leather soft.

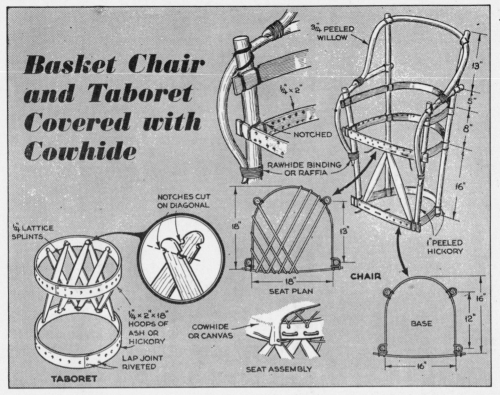

Basket Chair and Taboret Covered with Cowhide

Date-palm fronds are used in this Mexican original, but ¼″ splints may be easier to obtain.

MEXICAN craftsmen introduced this patio furniture to the Southwest. Working with primitive tools and materials, they have managed to fashion such comfortable and eye-appealing pieces that the supply of imported chairs and taborets like those illustrated has fallen hopelessly behind the demand. If you have a spot in your porch or garden that calls for this rustic furniture; you'll find that the quickest way to fill the vacancy is to build it yourself.

The drawing shows a simplified adaptation of the original; it can be made with jackknife, saw, and hand drill. Willow withes or other flexible branches that may be picked up in the woods are ideal for the frame. Hickory or ash should be used for the seat and base hoops, and ¼″ lattice splints for the diagonals that join them. Rawhide or raffia, and cowhide or canvas, in any combination, serve for the lacing and seat and back.

Soak or steam the ash or hickory and bend it around a rough form to make the three semicircular hoops needed for the chair. Bind them to the four legs with rawhide or raffia set in casein glue or shellac. The curved top frame and arms are installed next, and the diagonal slats are bound inside the hoops as shown. Rawhide strips are crisscrossed over the seat to support the cowhide or canvas cover, which is then fitted and laced in place. Seat and back are cut separately, and each piece is laced tightly in its frame.—HI SIBLEY.

The baby's play pen sketched below blends into a garden setting better than the ordinary painted inclosure. Details of the joints are shown at right

SIDE RAILS END RAILS SPINDLES 3/4" x 28"
SMOOTH BARK
28"
34"
NAILS
42"
8 HOOKS 2½" LONG
2"
1¼"
42"
8 ROUNDHEAD BOLTS, ¼" x 3"

A Rustic

PLAY PEN

for the Lawn

WHEN used outdoors in the garden or at a summer camp, the ordinary type of baby's play pen, being light colored and conspicuous, is less appropriate than one made of rustic materials like that illustrated.

To construct such a play pen, the following are required: 4 posts from 1½ to 2 in. in diameter and 34 in. long; 8 rails of the same diameter and 42 in. long; from 32 to 36 spindles from ¾ to 1 in. in diameter and 28 in. long; 8 hooks 2½ in. long with the necessary eyes or staples; and 8 roundhead bolts 3 by ¼ in. All the wood should be straight and have reasonably smooth bark.

Match the rails for each end and side, putting the lighter ones at the top. Dress down the ends of the rails that are to be used for the two end assemblies so they will enter ⅞-in. holes in the posts. Lay out equally spaced holes in the rails for the spindles. Bore the holes with a ¾-in. bit and assemble and nail the two end assemblies and the two side assemblies. Then bore ⅞-in. holes 2 in. from the bottom of the posts to receive the lower rails of the end assemblies. By putting the

lower rails in these holes, it can be seen where to bore the holes for the top rails. Put on the posts, drive the end assemblies together, and nail.

Leave the ends of the side rails square and bore holes endwise into them large enough to allow a ¼-in. bolt to enter easily. Mark up 1¼ in. from the bottom of the posts and bore ¼-in. holes corresponding to the holes in the lower side rails; then drive a 3 by ¼ in. bolt into each post from the outside to serve as dowel pins. Bore the upper holes through the posts to match the holes in the ends of the upper side rails, and put in similar bolts. Assemble the entire play pen and add the eight 2½ in. long safety hooks as shown in the drawing.

I oiled and varnished the one I built, and, besides being sturdy and weatherproof for outdoor use, it is fine enough even to use inside. It can be taken down and set up in a couple of minutes.

If thought necessary, a floor can be added by cutting lumber long enough to extend beyond the bottom end rails and nailing 1 by 2 in. cleats on the floor outside the rails.—A. C. SHUMAKER.

A TROPICAL LAWN CHAIR

Bamboo rug poles and sisal binder twine are two tropical materials that are within reach of almost everyone, even in the northern parts of the country, at very small cost. These two materials can be combined in building this strong and comfortable porch or lawn chair.

The bamboo poles can be obtained at almost any department or home-furnishing store as the larger rugs come rolled around these poles. They should be about 1 in. in diameter, and four 9-ft. poles are required. The binder (sisal) twine, which is used in reapers for tying up grain, may be purchased at any farm supply store.

Cut the poles as follows: two front legs, 25¼ in.; two back legs, 39 in.; two arms, 21 in.; three crosspieces, 23 in.; two seat rails, 19½ in.; two side braces, 35½ in. A hack saw is best to use in sawing up the poles.

Roundhead stove bolts are used for fastening the parts together. Fourteen of these are required 2½ by ¼ in., and two 3½ by ¼ in. A ¼-in. metal drill is used to make the holes with, and care must be used not to split the poles. All end holes are drilled 3 in. from the end. The bolts are drawn up snugly but not so tightly as to crack the poles. Twisted wires brace

Bamboo poles and sisal binder twine, costing but a trifle, are the materials for this chair

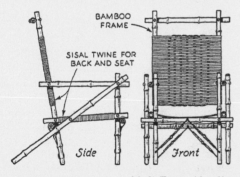

How the chair is assembled. To avoid splitting, a hack saw is used to cut up the poles

the chair sideways as illustrated.

The bamboo side braces are purposely made about 2 in. too long, for they must be cut to their proper length after the chair is completed. Bamboo is a rather irregular material to work with.

The space for the seat is completely filled with the twine, which is tightly wrapped around the side rails from front to back. The back of the chair is wrapped to within 4 in. of the top and bottom crosspieces.

The back and seat are now woven with seven cross twines by means of a long wire needle. The center one is woven in first and the others are woven around this until seven twines are in place.

Sisal binder twine is rather fuzzy and bristly, and when the weaving is completed it must be singed off with a blowtorch. This leaves a smooth, even finish to the hand-woven material of seat and back.—Harold Jackson.

RUSTIC NAME POST

ATTRACTIVE name and house-number boards can be made of scrap lumber and a tree branch or sapling log. A crossbar and brace made from a branch support the name board, which is suspended with short lengths of rope run through heavy screw eyes. Remove the bark from the end of the post that goes into the ground. Paint this with creosote to prevent decay.

Use a smooth board with jagged ends and leave it unpainted. Carve the lettering with a V-shaped chisel, paint it dark brown, and apply two coats of outdoor spar varnish. A color effect is obtained by burning the board slightly, brushing with a wire brush, and painting the letters Chinese red.

Rustic Trellis to Shade Door or Window

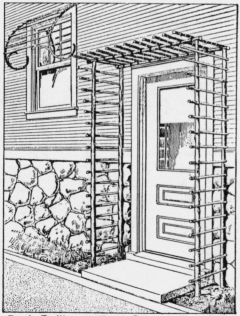

Rustic Trellises are Easily Constructed and When Covered with Vines Add to the Attractiveness of the Home

Proper preparation in the early spring will make it possible for the householder to shade doors and windows from the hot summer's sun by means of inexpensive rustic trellises that add not a little to the beauty of the home. A suggestion for a trellis at a doorway and one for a window are shown in the illustration. They are made of straight tree trunks and small limbs, having the bark on them. The curved portions of the window trellis may be made easily by using twigs that are somewhat green. Morning-glories, or other suitable climbing plants, may be trained over the trellises.—J. G. Allshouse, Avonmore, Pa.

FIGURE 5. PORCH SEAT OF BIRCH BRANCHES

While still outside the house it is a good time to consider a porch seat. Rustic seats are always good, and they require no great amount of skill in making. This one (Figure 5) is of birch branches. There is nothing quite so pretty as the birch with its curling silver bark, but there is always one objection to it, and that is, that the worms like to work in it better than in some other woods. For this, as for the screen, any kind of wood may be used—hickory, beech, oak, whatever happens to be growing most plentifully near your cottage. It is always a good idea to use a smooth board for the seat of one of those benches, as it is easier on the clothing. Beginning with this board, nail to its four sides four fairly straight sticks of birch. Fasten this at the two back corners to sticks that will bring the back of the seat as high as you like. Then put on the front legs, with cross-pieces for arms, and the building up of the back and the putting in of braces may be done as is most convenient. The braces, put in at angles, give a slant at the ends of the sticks that makes it easy to drive nails through.

So-called "rustic" window-boxes, decorated with branches, are much more attractive than the ordinary green or brown painted ones, and are interesting to make. Different kinds of branches, such as birch, cherry, and pine, can be used.

The boxes themselves can be of various shapes and sizes, though the kind generally preferred is a narrow box with a length equal to, or a little shorter than, that of the window in front of which it is to be placed. Other types of boxes, shorter in length and with a greater width are, however, frequently used.

When a suitable box has been picked out, make sure that it is well fastened together. Put in more nails if they are needed. Then drill four ½-inch holes in the bottom to allow the excess water to drain off.

The rustic trimming is provided by small, straight branches nailed to the sides and ends of the box in an upright position. If you wish, you can add binding-pieces at the top and bottom. These are long pieces of wood and are nailed in place as shown in the drawing. This type of trimming harmonizes beautifully with the plants in the box. After the branches are all in place, they should be given a coat of varnish in order to preserve them against water and rotting, and also to improve their appearance.

A VERY attractive hanging flower-box which, when filled with plants, will bring pleasure the year around, can be made with very little effort.

The chief requisite is a shallow, wooden grocery box of the type shown in the illustration. To the bottom of this box, nail two strips of wood. Each strip should be 1 inch wide and ½ inch deep, and each should be 2 inches longer than the width of the box. These are to serve as hangers, and their function is to take the weight of the earth with which the box is filled off the bottom boards of the box itself.

Four screw-eyes are screwed into the ends of these cross strips, and four lengths of wire are twisted into the screw-eyes. The free ends of the wires are then brought together and twisted around each other so they will bear the weight of the box. A short piece of wire, bent into the shape of a circle, is passed beneath the four main wires where they join together. The ends of the short wire are then twisted tightly together so a loop is formed by which to hang up the flower-box.

When completed, the flower-box may be painted dark green or brown, or else be made into a "rustic" box by covering it with small, straight pieces of branches, fastened to the sides of the box with small nails.

HANGING FERN BASKET

A very pretty hanging basket may be made by building up small straight sticks with the bark on in the same way that a log house is built. The  size of the basket will depend largely on the size of the fern which you wish to grow, but ordinarily the sticks should be from twelve to sixteen inches long. The sizes should taper from an inch in diameter for those at the bottom to half an inch for the top ones. In starting the construction, nail four of the larger sticks together, so as to make a frame with the ends projecting about one and a half to two inches. Between the two upper sticks place a row of sticks so as to form a grating with half-inch spaces. This makes the bottom, and in building up the sides we simply nail on two pieces running one way and then two running the other, until the desired height is reached. Always drive the nails in at an angle, so that the nails of the next layer will not interfere when they are put in. The best plan is to have the sticks all sawn to the proper length before nailing together, so that the

entire attention may be given to building the sides
up squarely. Two long, thin branches are now to
be found and slowly bent so as to form the long
handles. Nail these to the inside corners, and wire
the handles together at. the top—and the basket is
done.

In filling such a basket with new earth it will
be necessary to line the inside with moss or leaves
·to keep it in, but after a few waterings the whole
forms into a solid mass and no trouble will be
found.

GARDEN ARCHES

The
arch at Fig. 1 is made from so-called rustic wood,
actually it is larch or fir, with the bark left on the poles.
Suitable dimensions for the arch are given at Fig. 2, and
included at Fig. 3 are details of the joints. At least
4 ft. of the upright poles should be buried in the ground.

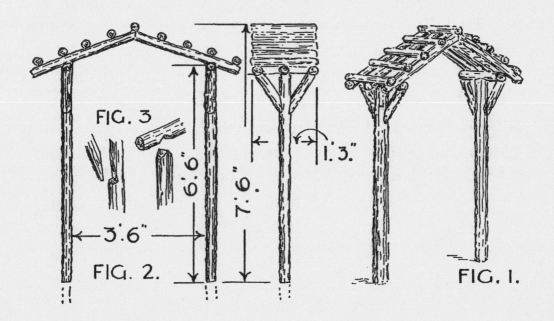

FIG. 3

FIG. 2.

FIG. 1.

6'.6"

7'.6"

3'.6"

1'.3."

To plant flowers in a stiff looking box, a tin can or a pail, is to lose half their lovely effect when they are in bloom.   We should always try to pro-

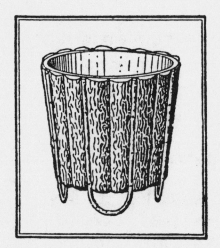

vide an attractive place for them, because much of the time the plants have no flowers and no one wishes to have an ugly box or a rusty pail standing around.

A rustic tub is suitable for large plants or even small trees, and is very easily made.   Take a small tub such as butter comes in or else a wooden pail without a handle and cover the outside with slabs of wood about two inches wide with the bark on.   These may be sawn from branches from three to four inches in diameter. Have them all exactly the same length and fitted closely together so that the tub is entirely hidden. If you can find some green boughs about one-half inch in diameter that will stand to be slowly bent half way around a tin can, our tub may be pro- vided with feet, as shown in the drawing.   In this case a space must be left between every other or every third slab, and the number and width of the slabs should be arranged so that the feet will come out right.

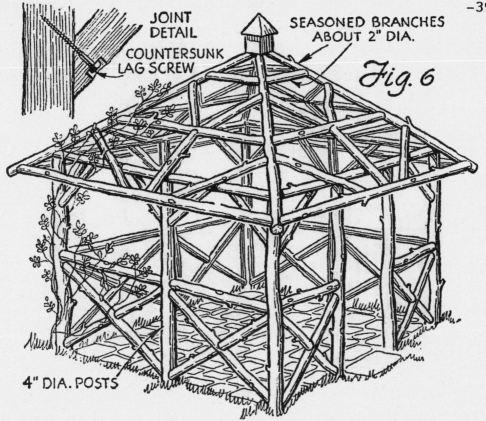

JOINT DETAIL

COUNTERSUNK LAG SCREW

SEASONED BRANCHES ABOUT 2" DIA.

Fig. 6

4" DIA. POSTS

a rustic arbor made from well-seasoned tree branches or sapling logs in Fig. 6. The bark may be left on the logs used for the latter if it is a variety that clings after becoming dry.

Log Flower Holders

GIVE a rustic atmosphere to the living room or porch with several of these willow or log flower and pot holders. Four suggestions are shown in the drawing, two of them being log holders and the others willow-covered jars or boxes for potted plants or cut flowers.

The log bowl is a log slab, from 7" to 11" in diameter and about 4½" or 5" deep, with the bark cut away around t h e lower part, and turned on the lathe as shown. The inside of the bowl is cut out to a depth of

two or three inches as indicated in the cross section, suitable f o r holding shallow pans or containers. If desired, the bowl can be filled with earth and seeds or bulbs planted, d r a i n holes being bored in the

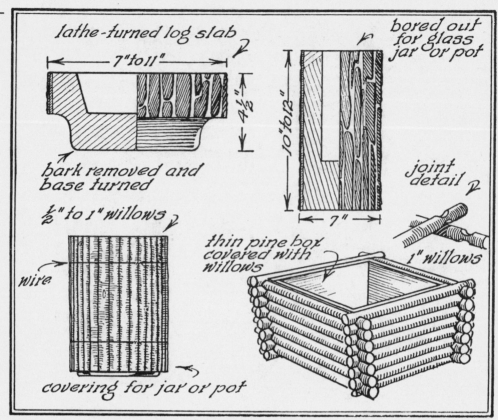

lathe-turned log slab

7" to 11"

4½"

bark removed and base turned

½" to 1" willows

wire

covering for jar or pot

bored out for glass jar or pot

10" to 12"

7"

joint detail

1" willows

thin pine box covered with willows

bottom and the slab set in a shallow tin pan. The vertical log has the center bored and cut out to take a glass bottle or jar for cut flowers.

Lacquer the wood where it is exposed thru the bark, or paint or stain it brown. A rustic cover of willow sections, from ½" to 1" thick, can be cut, trimmed and fastened about the straight-sided pot or jar with two strands of wire clamped around the willows and secured with the ends twisted together.

A fourth holder consists of a box made from thin pine boards, nailed together as shown and covered with

1" willows, joined at the corners in log-cabin style. Allow willow lengths 3½" or 4" longer than the length of the box which they cover, cutting two notches in each willow near the end and setting them together at right angles. Drive a small nail thru each joint as the rows of willows are laid around the box.

LOG BOWLS

TURN out some of these rustic log bowls on your lathe, and use them for fruit, candy or nuts. You will want them for holidays and other occasions. Farmers often have hardwood logs, such as walnut, hickory, oak and maple, which they use during the winter. Select two or three short lengths, making sure they are as well seasoned as possible, and with an adhering bark for bark-trimmed bowls.

Four types of bowls are shown, which are but a few of many designs you may turn out easily on the lathe. One has the bark removed, while the others are with narrow or wide bark trim. Saw out blocks or slabs to fit approximately the size of the bowl you wish. Trim the bark edge carefully with a chisel, later marking it as it turns in the lathe, and finishing with a hand chisel. Avoid the bark when turning down the bowl in the lathe, since it is apt to tear off. Cut a neat bevel around the upper edge, and turn down a neat base, with ornamental beading.

The thickness of the bowls is suggested in cross-section diagrams, being hollowed out on the lathe and finished at the bottom with a chisel by hand. Leave the bowls natural, or hold a stained cloth against the wood when it is turning. A burned beading can be had by holding a folded cloth tightly against the spinning bead.

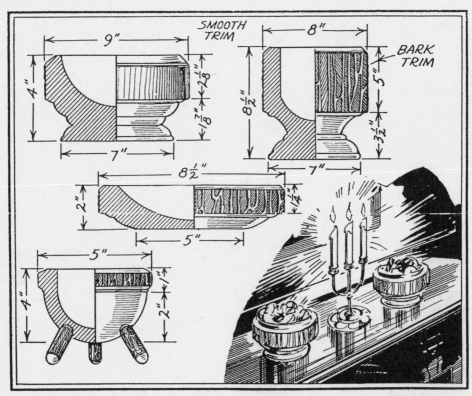

HOUSES MADE OF POLES
BY LOLA A. PINCHON

[In this article descriptions are given of several shelters suitable for a resort, but the reader may select any one of them that answers his needs and build a camp house, or fit up a more substantial one to make living quarters for the whole year.—Editor.]

BEING forced to take the open-air treatment to regain health, a person adopted the plan of building a pole house in the woods, and the scheme was so successful that it was decided to make a resort grounds, to attract crowds during holidays, by which an income could be realized for living expenses. All the pavilions, stands, furniture, and amusement devices were constructed of straight poles cut from young growth of timber with the bark remaining on them. Outside of boards for flooring and roofing material, the entire construction of the buildings and fences consisted of poles.

A level spot was selected and a house built having three rooms. The location was in a grove of young timbers, most of it being straight, and 13 trees were easily found that would make posts 12 ft. long, required for the sides, and two poles 16 ft. long, for the center of the ends, so that they would reach to the ridge. The plot was laid out rectangular and marked for the poles, which were set in the ground for a depth of 4 ft., at distances of 6 ft. apart. This made the house 8 ft. high at the eaves with a square pitch roof; that is, the ridge was 3 ft. high in the center from the plate surfaces for this width of a house. The rule for finding this height is to take one-quarter of the width of

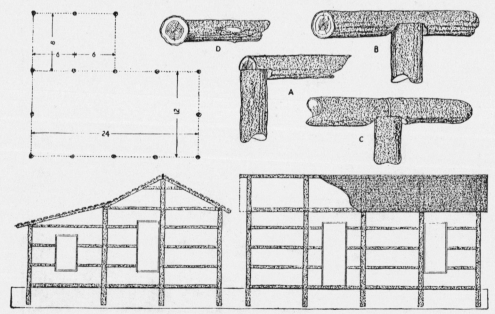

The Frame Construction of the House Made Entirely of Rough Poles, the Verticals being Set in the Ground, Plumbed, and Sighted to Make a Perfect Rectangle of the Desired Proportions

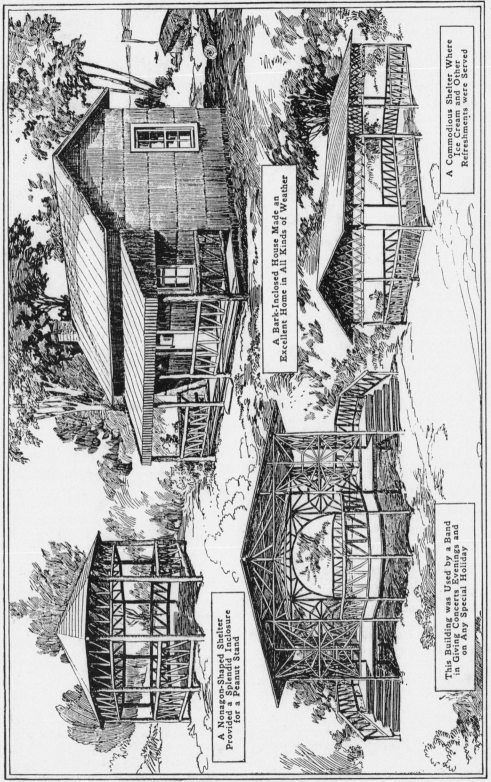

A Bark-Inclosed House Made an Excellent Home in All Kinds of Weather

A Commodious Shelter Where Ice Cream and Other Refreshments were Served

A Nonagon-Shaped Shelter Provided a Splendid Inclosure for a Peanut Stand

This Building was Used by a Band in Giving Concerts Evenings and on Any Special Holiday

the house for the height in the center from the plate.

The corner poles were carefully lo-

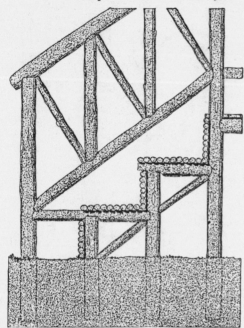

The Steps are Supported on Pairs of Vertical Poles Set in the Ground to Make Different Levels

cated to make the size 12 by 24 ft., with a lean-to 8 by 12 ft., and then plumbed to get them straight vertically. The plates for the sides, consisting of five poles, were selected as straight as possible and their ends and centers hewn down to about one-half their thickness, as shown at A and B, and nailed to the tops of the vertical poles, the connection for center poles being as shown at C.

The next step was to secure the vertical poles with crosspieces between them which were used later for supporting the siding. These poles were cut about 6 ft. long, their ends being cut concave to fit the curve of the upright poles, as shown at D. These were spaced evenly, about 2 ft. apart from center to center, on the sides and ends, as shown in the sketch, and toenailed in place. The doors and window openings were cut in the horizontal poles wherever wanted, and casements set in and nailed. The first row of horizontal poles was placed close to the ground

and used both as support for the lower ends of the siding and to nail the ends of the flooring boards to, which were fastened in the center to poles laid on stones, or, better still, placed on top of short blocks, 5 ft. long, set in the ground. These poles for the floor should be placed not over 2 ft. apart to make the flooring solid.

A lean-to was built by setting three poles at a distance of 8 ft. from one side, beginning at the center and extending to the end of the main building. These poles were about 6 ft. long above the ground. The rafter poles for this part were about 9½ ft. long, notched at both ends for the plates, the ends of the house rafters being sawed off even with the outside of the plate along this edge. The rafter poles for the house were 10 in all, 8 ft. long, and were laid off and cut to fit a ridge made of a board. These poles were notched about 15 in. from their lower ends to fit over the rounding edge of the plate pole, and were then placed directly over each vertical wall pole. They were nailed both to the plate and to the ridge, also further strengthened by a brace made of a piece of board or a

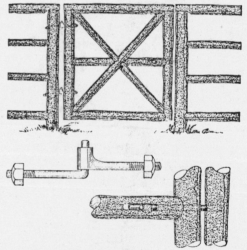

Gate Openings were Made in the Fence Where Necessary, and Gates of Poles Hung in the Ordinary Manner

small pole, placed under the ridge and nailed to both rafters. On top of the rafters boards were placed horizontally, spaced about 1 ft. apart, but this is optional with the builder, as other roofing material can be used. In this instance metal roofing was used, and railing. It is very easy to make ornamental parts, such as shown, on the eave of the porch, by splitting sticks

All Furniture, Together with the Large Lawn Swings, Took on the General Appearance of the Woodland, and As the Pieces were Made Up of the Same Material As the Houses, the Cost Was Only the Labor and a Few Nails

it only required fastening at intervals, and to prevent rusting out, it was well painted on the under side before laying it and coated on the outside when fastened in place. If a more substantial shelter is wanted, it is best to lay the roof solid with boards, then cover it with the regular prepared roofing material.

Some large trees were selected and felled, then cut into 4-ft. lengths and the bark removed, or if desired, the bark removed in 4-ft. lengths, and nailed on the outside of the poles, beginning at the bottom in the same manner as laying shingles, to form the siding of the house. If a more substantial house is wanted, boards can be nailed on the poles, then the bark fastened to the boards; also, the interior can be finished in wall board.

The same general construction is used for the porch, with horizontal poles latticed, as shown, to form the

and nailing them on closely together to make a frieze. Floors are laid on the porch and in the house, and doors hung and window sash fitted in the same manner as in an ordinary house.

A band stand was constructed on sloping ground, and after setting the poles, the floor horizontals were placed about 2 ft. above the ground, on the upper side, and 4 ft. on the lower side. The poles used were about 18 ft. long. Instead of having the horizontals 2 ft. apart, the first was placed 1 ft. above the floor, the next at about one-half the distance from the lower one to the plate at the top, and the space between was ornamented with cross poles, as shown. A balcony or bay was constructed at one end, and a fancy roof was made of poles whose ends rested on a curved pole attached to the vertical pieces. Steps were formed of several straight poles, hewn down on their ends to make a level place to rest on horizontal pieces attached to stakes at the ends. A pair of stakes were used at each end of a step, and these were fastened to a slanting piece at the top, their lower ends being set into the ground. The manner of bracing and crossing with horizontals makes a rigid form of construction, and if choice poles are selected for the step pieces, they will be comparatively level and of sufficient strength to hold up all the load put on them. The roof of this building was made for a sun

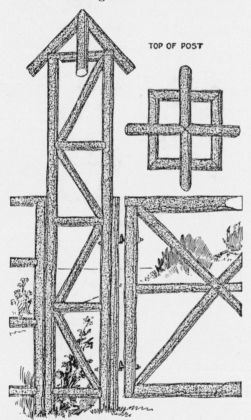

TOP OF POST

The Entrance to the Grounds was Given an Inviting Appearance with Large Posts and Swinging Gates

shade only and consisted of boards nailed closely together on the rafters.

An ice-cream parlor was built on the same plan, but without any board floor; the ground, being level, was used instead. There were five vertical poles used for each end with a space left between the two poles at the center, on both sides, for an entrance. This building was covered with prepared roofing,

so that the things kept for sale could be protected in case of a shower.

A peanut stand was also built without a floor, and to make it with nine sides, nine poles were set in the ground to form a perfect nonagon and joined at their tops with latticed horizontals. Then a rafter was run from the top of each post to the center, and boards were fitted on each pair of rafters over the V-shaped openings. The boards were then covered with prepared roofing. A railing was formed of horizontals set in notches, cut in the posts, and then ornamented in the same manner as for the other buildings.

Fences were constructed about the grounds, made of pole posts with horizontals on top, hewn down and fitted as the plates for the house; and the lower pieces were set in the same as for making the house railing. Gates were made of two vertical pieces, the height of the posts, and two horizontals, then braced with a piece running from the lower corner at the hinge side to the upper opposite corner, the other cross brace being joined to the sides of the former, whereupon two short horizontals were fitted in the center. A blacksmith formed some hinges of rods and strap iron, as shown, and these were fastened in holes bored in the post and the gate vertical. A latch was made by boring a hole through the gate vertical and into the end of the short piece. Then a slot was cut in the side to receive a pin inserted in a shaft made to fit the horizontal hole. A keeper was made in the post by boring a hole to receive the end of the latch.

Large posts were constructed at the entrance to the grounds, and on these double swing gates, made up in the same manner as the small one, were attached. These large posts were built up of four slender poles and were considerably higher than the fence poles. The poles were set in a perfect square, having sides about 18 in. long, and a square top put on by mitering the corners, whereupon four small rafters were fitted on top. The gates were swung on hinges made like those for the small gate.

Among the best and most enjoyed amusement devices on the grounds were the swings. Several of these were built, with and without tables. Four poles, about 20 ft. long, were set in the ground at an angle, and each pair of side poles was joined with two horizontals, about 12 ft. long, spreaders being fastened between the two horizontals to keep the tops of the poles evenly spaced. The distance apart of the poles will depend on the size of the swing and the number of persons to be seated. Each pair of side poles are further strengthened with crossed poles, as shown. If no table is to be used in the swing, the poles may be set closer together, so that the top horizontals will be about 8 ft. long. The platform for the swinging part consists of two poles, 12 ft. long, which are swung on six vertical poles, about 14 ft. long. These poles are attached to the top hor-izontals with long bolts, or rods, running through both, the bottom being attached in the same manner. Poles are nailed across the platform horizontals at the bottom for a floor, and a table with seats at the ends is formed of poles. The construction is obvious.

A short space between two trees can be made into a seat by fastening two horizontals, one on each tree, with the ends supported by braces. Poles are nailed on the upper surface for a seat.

Other furniture for the house and grounds was made of poles in the manner illustrated. Tables were built for picnickers by setting four or six poles in the ground and making a top of poles or boards. Horizontals were placed across the legs with extending ends, on which seats were made for the tables. Chairs and settees were built in the same manner, poles being used for the entire construction.

Graceful Rustic Bench for Lawn or Garden

ALMOST any kind of logs can be used to build this substantial rustic bench for the lawn. The corner posts are 36 in. high and about 5 in. in diameter. The rest of the logs are smaller—about 3 in. at the large end. The two lower rails are notched into the corner posts or legs as shown. The logwork at the back is marked and fitted one piece at a time.

All joints are spiked with care to prevent splitting. It is a good idea to drill holes wherever the spikes have to be placed close to the ends. At all major points twenty-penny spikes should be used, but sixteen-penny can be used at the smaller joints.

The seat is made of two planks 2 in. thick, 10 in. wide, and 6 ft. long. These are supported by a piece of "2 by 4" at each end, which is spiked to the legs. The seat planks are notched into the legs slightly, and the ends are capped over with a half log as shown in the seat detail. Half of the log is used at each end.

The seat, ends of all logs, and places where branches have been cut off may be painted some bright color. Orange, red, or light green are suitable colors to use.—H.J.

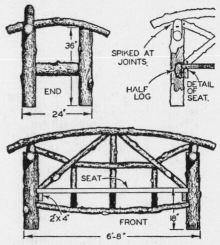

Curved logs are used for the main back rail and the arms to give the bench individuality

A Tree Hut and Rustic Shelter of Poles and Brushwood

By EDWARD A. KRUEGER

IRRESISTIBLE is the lure of autumn's days to the woodsman, young or old, calling him forth over a carpet of fallen leaves, to roam or hunt, with a companion or two, in the quiet of the woods. As if in anticipation of winter's rigors, it is the season for the building of a rustic hut, a shelter from the elements. For the younger woodsmen, at least, this becomes a romantic retreat, a storied scout's camp of older days, or a secret rendezvous of warring Indians, perhaps. A novel woods shelter of unusual construction, that boys can build with only a few tools, is a tree hut of timber poles and brushwood. It may be supported by a single large tree, or by two or more trees. In the latter case, the framework may be built around the trees, or between them, depending on their relative position. The octagonal tree house, shown in the sketch, is strongly framed. The joints are bolted, or spiked, together, and the weight is carried by the main-floor beams, firmly braced against the tree trunk. Round poles and brush sticks, as they are gathered or cut in the

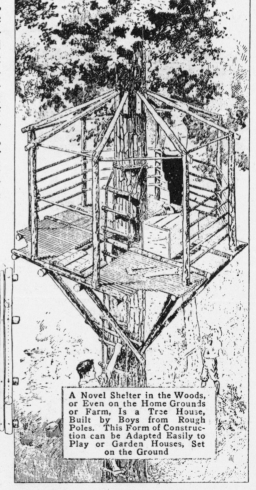

A Novel Shelter in the Woods, or Even on the Home Grounds or Farm, Is a Tree House, Built by Boys from Rough Poles. This Form of Construction can be Adapted Easily to Play or Garden Houses, Set on the Ground

woods, are used throughout. The construction can, of course, be carried out with standard mill stock, 2 by 4-in. stuff being used for the heavier timbers; 2 by 2-in., for the rafters, and 1-in. strips and boards, for the floor and the smaller braces.

The same general method of framing, omitting unnecessary features, can be adapted to an octagonal hut built around the base of a tree. On clear ground, where no central support is available, the roof rafters can be braced around a short section of timber, about 6 in. in diameter. The ground framing may consist only of sills, extending around the octagonal outline, with or without a floor. Built on the ground, a structure of this type can serve as a rustic garden shelter, as a children's playhouse, or even for the more common purpose of a storage shed.

The dimensions of the framing may vary, within safe limits, and the sizes suggested are suitable for a tree about 2 ft. in diameter. The octagon, on which the framing for the floor is laid out, as shown in the plan, has a 4-ft. radius. This is a safe maximum for the type of construction shown, for if the main timbers are made longer, it is difficult to support them properly from a single tree trunk. To make the main framework for the floor, cut four poles, A, 3 in. in diameter and 8 ft. long, as scaled from the plan. To obtain dimensions from the plan readily, make a strip of paper, 1 in. wide and as long as the heavy floor supports. Divide this length into eight parts, each of which will represent 1 ft. on the construction. If the tree is of uniform diameter, near the ground and at the point where the floor frame is supported, the frame may be bolted together firmly on the ground, and hoisted into place. Otherwise, it should be fitted together on the ground, and not bolted finally until in place. The timbers are supported by four blocks, nailed to the trunk at the point where the frame is to be set. It is further held in place by spikes.

If bolts are used at the main joints of the frame, the pieces may all be cut and fitted on the ground, and then raised and put into place finally, one at a time. Cut two pieces, B, 2½ in. in diameter and 5 ft. long; two pieces, C, 2½ in. by 5½ ft. long; and two pieces, D, 2½ in. by 8 ft. long. The pieces D are bolted under the pieces C, and two of the pieces A are set slightly nearer the other pieces A, than the pieces B. When the main frame is in place, brace it from the trunk, the notches for the ends of the braces being cut into two of the pieces A, 8 in. from their ends, on the ground. The corresponding ends of the braces are sharpened to a wedge to fit them, and spiked into place. The braces that are notched into two of the pieces A are parallel, as shown, their lower ends being spiked to the sides of the trunk. The two braces on each of the other two braced sides are not parallel. They are notched into the pieces B, and spiked, at the notches and at the junction with the trunk, just above the parallel braces.

The climbing ladder, of rope and short sections of 1½-in. poles, can be made on the ground and hoisted into place. It is spread from the trunk at the top and at intervals by short sticks, spiked to the trunk. The ladder is arranged so that it can be drawn up into the house, if desired. The floor of the platform is made of poles, 1½ to 2 in. in diameter, arranged across the timbers, as shown, and nailed in place. It is important that the poles for the floor be extended well beyond the beams, as indicated, so that no long, free ends of the poles project. The trapdoor is made of 1-in. lumber, braced with two cleats. It is hinged on strips of leather, and arranged so that its ends rest on the adjoining beams A. It is shown closed, in the plan, and open, in the sketch.

The sides and roof of the house are supported by 2½-in. poles, for studding, and 2-in. poles, for the rafters. They are cut on the ground, and the joints at the eaves halved, and bolted, or spiked, as shown. The upper ends of the rafters are set on wooden strips, nailed to the trunk at a uniform height, and spiked in place. The studding and rafters are braced with smaller poles, extending around the octagon at the top, and around the inside, as a guard against the occupants of the house falling out.

The tree hut can be covered in various ways. To carry out the rustic effect completely, the roof and sides may be thatched with twigs and brush. If the house is used only during fairly moderate weather, a latticework of small poles is satisfactory, and a canvas roof may be used. The sides may also be covered with canvas, and the entire structure may be boarded over, leaving, in each case, sufficient openings for light.

to the front rail and also connected to the back post by a bearer, 4 in. deep by $1\frac{1}{2}$ in. thick. This bearer is tenoned to the back post.

Fig. 3 shows a sectional view of the bearer joint to front leg, and also the half-round seat battens resting on the bearer, also showing them with their edges planed. It is advisable to have a space between the edges of each batten, say about $\frac{1}{8}$ in., to allow rainwater to drain. The ends of the seat battens are pared away to fit the transverse rails neatly as shown in Fig. 2. The struts for the post range in diameter from $1\frac{1}{2}$ in. to 2 in. The ends of the struts are pared to fit the posts and

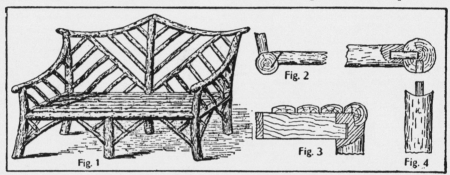

Rustic Seat and Details of Construction

How to Make a Rustic Seat

The rustic settee illustrated in Fig. 1 may be made 6 ft. long, which will accommodate four average-sized persons. It is not advisable to exceed this length, as then it would look out of proportion, says the Wood-Worker. Select the material for the posts, and for preference branches that are slightly curved, as shown in the sketch. The front posts are about $3\frac{1}{2}$ in. in diameter by 2 ft. 4 in. long. The back posts are 3 ft. 4 in. high, while the center post is 3 ft. 8 in. in height. The longitudinal and transverse rails are about 3 in. in diameter and their ends are pared away to fit the post to which they are connected by 1-in. diameter dowels. This method is shown in Fig. 4. The dowel holes are bored at a distance of 1 ft. $2\frac{1}{2}$ in, up from the lower ends of posts. The front center leg is partially halved

rails, and are then secured with two or three brads at each end.

Select curved pieces, about $2\frac{1}{2}$ in. in diameter, for the arm rests and back rails; while the diagonally placed filling may be about 2 in. in diameter. Start with the shortest lengths, cutting them longer than required, as the paring necessary to fit them to the rails and posts shortens them a little. Brad them in position as they are fitted, and try to arrange them at regular intervals.

Rustic Crow's Nest Beautifies Dead Tree

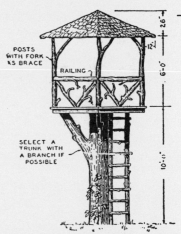

Don't cut a dead tree down to the base. Make it a support for a rustic crow's nest, as shown.

A LARGE shade tree is an asset even after it dies, if conveniently located, for upon its trunk a very attractive rustic crow's nest can be built, high enough above the ground to catch all the breezes and to give a splendid view of the surrounding territory.

The summer house can be adapted to almost any tree trunk. If there is any choice, select one which has a branch to serve as a brace. Other braces are fastened to the dead trunk with lag screws.

The height above the ground depends, of course, upon the location and size of the trunk; ten feet is about right. Prepare the trunk by sawing off level and hewing two shoulders to support the main floor joists.

A modification of the crow's nest here shown, makes an ideal camping home for the summer, amid lofty trees, or overlooking the sea. For such purpose, build the walls solid.

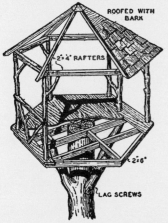

Constructional details are given in this diagram.

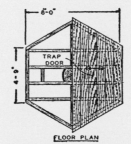

Showing the bracing of the floor.

How the thatched roof is made.

With these as a foundation the remaining joists and sills can be assembled over braces of rough branches. Chop a notch or step in the tree trunk for each brace, and fasten them to it with lag screws.

Lay the floor over the joists and proceed with the uprights and rafters. For the uprights select rough branches, preferably with forks near the top. In rustic work of this kind it is best to allow the wood to season a few months so that there will be no shrinkage after assembly.

Cover the roof sheathing with roll roofing, and shingle with seasoned bark, or cover with straw matting in the manner illustrated. A rustic rail further braces the structure, and a rustic ladder is built up the tree trunk, access being through a trap door. Reed furniture and grass rugs are appropriate for this inviting retreat, and Japanese lanterns could easily be wired from the house circuit.—H. S.

Bird Houses For Your Garden

HERE are several designs for bird houses that should meet the requirements of almost any lover of birds. Among those shown, are colony houses, four-apartment log cabins and single-apartment homes of rustic design, which are made from short sections of logs. Essential dimensions in building bird houses are the sizes of the nesting compartment and the entrance hole, which are given in the table.

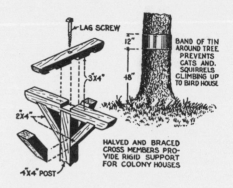

LAG SCREW

BAND OF TIN AROUND TREE PREVENTS CATS AND SQUIRRELS CLIMBING UP TO BIRD HOUSE

HALVED AND BRACED CROSS MEMBERS PROVIDE RIGID SUPPORT FOR COLONY HOUSES

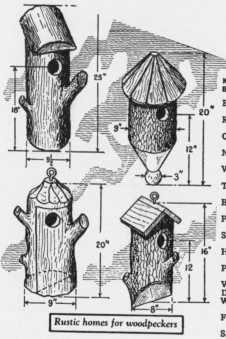

Rustic homes for woodpeckers

TABLE OF BIRD-HOUSE SIZES

Kind of Bird	Floor of Cavity	Depth of Cavity	Entrance Above Floor	Dia. of Entrance	Height above Ground (Ft.)
Bluebird	5 x 5	8	6	1½	5 to 10
Robin	6 x 8	8	2 adjacent sides open		6 to 15
Chickadee	4 x 4	8 to 10	8	1	6 to 15
Nuthatch	4 x 4	8 to 10	8	1¼	12 to 20
Wren	4 x 4	6 to 8	1 to 6	⅞	6 to 10
Tree Swallow	5 x 5	6	1 to 6	1½	10 to 15
Barn Swallow	6 x 6	6	2 adjacent sides open		8 to 12
Purple Martin	6 x 6	6	1	2½	15 to 20
Song Sparrow	6 x 6	6	3 sides open		2 to 4
House Finch	6 x 6	6	4	2	8 to 12
Phoebe	6 x 6	6	2 adjacent sides open		8 to 12
Woodpecker	6 x 6	12 to 15	12	1½ to 2	12 to 20
Downy Woodpecker	4 x 4	8 to 10	8	1¼	6 to 20
Flicker	7 x 7	16 to 18	16	2½	6 to 20
Screech Owl	8 x 8	12 to 15	12	3	10 to 30

The small frame houses and the log-cabin types should be colored with brown or green shingle stain, while white paint, with a harmonizing trim color, is best for colony houses. The latter should be mounted rigidly on a stout post, which is pivoted at the bottom so that they can be lowered for cleaning. Also, note that the colony houses have a built-in system of ventilation, which is essential. The construction of the rustic-bark homes is clearly shown.

Those made from single logs are ripped, and, after the cavity has been chiseled out, the halves are fastened together with wire or large screws. A thin coating of asbestos-roofing cement spread on the joining faces of the two halves will keep water out of the nesting cavity.

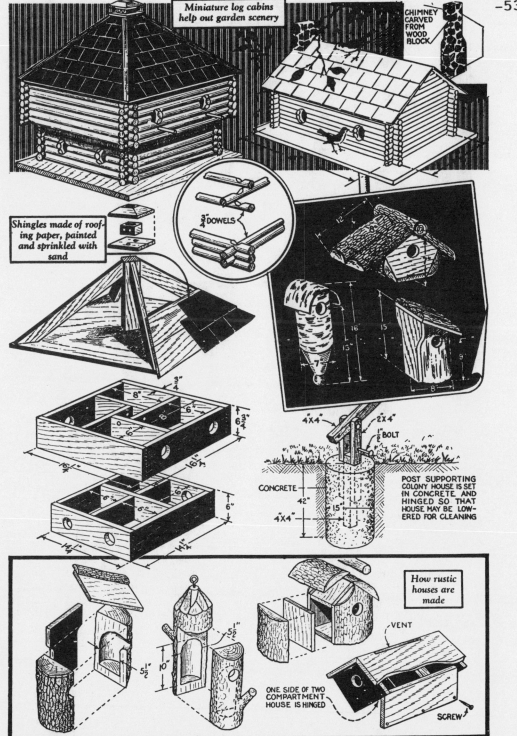

Miniature log cabins help out garden scenery

CHIMNEY CARVED FROM WOOD BLOCK

Shingles made of roofing paper, painted and sprinkled with sand

3/4" DOWELS

12

16"   15"

13"

7

8"   9"

3/4"

8"   6"

8"

6 3/4"

16 1/4"

6"

6"

6"

14 1/4"   14 1/4"

4"X4"   2"X4"

1/2" BOLT

CONCRETE

42"

15

4"X4"

POST SUPPORTING COLONY HOUSE IS SET IN CONCRETE AND HINGED SO THAT HOUSE MAY BE LOWERED FOR CLEANING

How rustic houses are made

1"
5 1/2

10"

5 1/2"

5 1/2"

VENT

ONE SIDE OF TWO COMPARTMENT HOUSE IS HINGED

SCREW

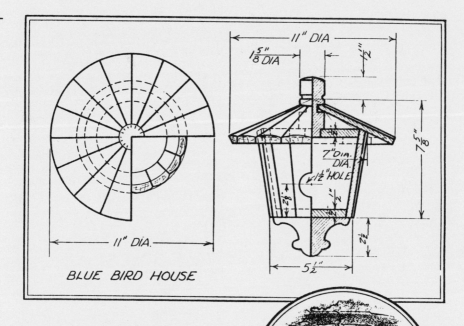

11" DIA

1 5/8" DIA

1/2"

7 5/8"

7" DIA.

1 1/2" HOLE

1/2

2"

2 1/2"

5 1/2"

11" DIA.

BLUE BIRD HOUSE

Blue Bird

The bluebird house should have an opening 1½" in diameter. An opening of this size will admit the sparrow (a most dangerous enemy of the bluebird). That the bluebird is almost extinct in some sections of the country is due almost entirely to the fighting characteristics of the sparrow.

The drawings given here show the various dimensions to be used in the construction of Bluebird houses. It will be observed that branches of trees have been sawed lengthwise and used in the construction of the bluebird house.

Of all the birds we have secured as tenants of our garden apartments we like the house wrens best. They are regular little alarm clocks, always full of life, and they "sing their heads off" from morning till night. Wrens are the least fastidious of nesting birds; anything from an old shoe to a tin can suits them, but they do appreciate a house built especially for them. The ideal wren house has a floor space 4 by 4 in., 6 to 8 in. deep, with the entrance from 1 to 5 in. above the floor. Up to a few years ago, the standard specifications for a wren-house entrance called for a round hole the size of a quarter (15/16 in.), and this seemed to suit the birds

a dark brown. The dimensions for this house are: ends 5 in. wide and 8 in. high, sides 8 to 10 in. long, and roof and floor to fit. Be sure to allow the roof to project in front and rear to keep the rain out, and waterproof the joint of the roof boards with a strip of roofing paper, tacked over it.

The type shown in Fig. 3 is a very attractive one, and is made very simply, using a piece of pine for the back and sawmill-waste slabs for the front, sides and roof. Proportion the box as specified before. The house in Fig. 4 is also very simple to make, either from plain boards or from rough slabs. Make the floor 10 in. long and 4 or 5 in. wide. The sloping sides of the box are 10 in. long.

(2)

very well. Now, however, the bird lover has taken into consideration the wren's habit of carrying into its box short sticks for the nest, and he specifies that the entrance shall be a horizontal slot, 3 in. long and as wide as a quarter. This enables the nest builder to get its sticks into the box without much trouble. This type of entrance is shown in the house in Fig. 4. In Figs. 2 and 3 are shown two other types of wren houses that can be adapted to other birds by simply changing the dimensions. The log-cabin type, in Fig. 2, is most easily built by using dowel sticks, ¾ in. in diameter, notching the corners as in regular log-cabin construction and either chinking the joints between the logs or lining the inside of the house with thin wallboard for warmth. The "logs" should be stained

(3)

(4)

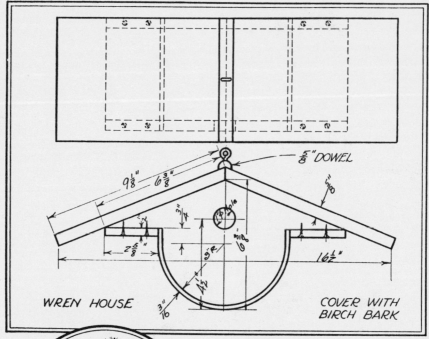

WREN HOUSE

$\frac{5}{8}$"DOWEL

COVER WITH BIRCH BARK

Furniture for the garden

Making a Rustic Table from a Forked Tree Trunk

MANY trees marked for firewood can serve the double purpose of furnishing the woodshed with fuel and the garden with an easily made rustic table.

At the point where the trunk divides into branches one can sometimes find a formation of three or four boughs spreading out in such a way that by cutting off level on top and bottom, the stand or base for a table may be made. A suitable board top is nailed to the support and, if desired, small branches split in two lengthwise can be nailed around the edges of the top.

The maple-tree is one of the best for furnishing these table legs.—A. E. ZIPPRICH.

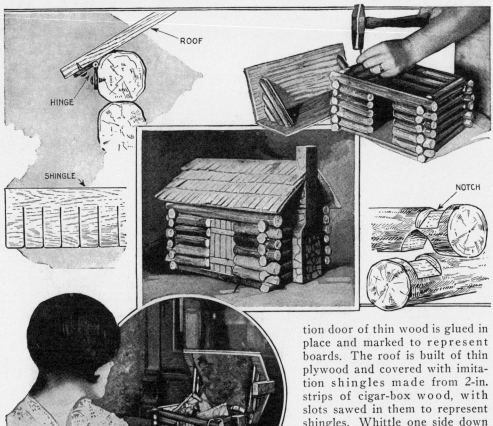

Resembling an old-fashioned log cabin, this jewel box is made from small green twigs, about ¾ or 1 in. thick, with the bark left on. Cut twelve pieces, 11 in. long, for the sides and an equal number, 8 in. long, for the ends, while varying sizes are used for the gables. The pieces for the sides and ends are notched deeply enough for the logs to fit closely together when fitted. The height of the sides, when assembled, should be about 6 in. The twigs are assembled by nailing them with lath nails, each to the one below it. Avoid nailing near the corners, or the pieces may split. The doorway is 2 in. wide, leaving the top and bottom logs intact. An imitation door of thin wood is glued in place and marked to represent boards. The roof is built of thin plywood and covered with imitation shingles made from 2-in. strips of cigar-box wood, with slots sawed in them to represent shingles. Whittle one side down to a wedge shape for the overlap of the next course. Cut the chimney from 1-in. material, and score and paint it to imitate rough stone. Nail it to the side of the cabin and cut it in two, so that the upper half will rise with the roof when the box is opened. Hinges complete the assembly. Wood filler is used to calk the cracks. A lining for the inside of the box can be made of cardboard which may be covered with fancy cloth. No paint or varnish should be used for the walls, but the roof, door and log ends should be stained to represent weathered wood.—Paul Hadley, Piggott, Ark.

RUSTIC DESIGN Features

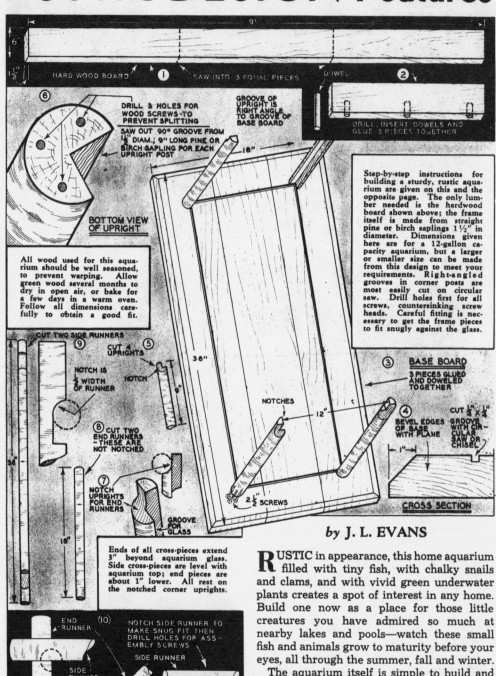

9'

6"

1½"

HARD WOOD BOARD ① SAW INTO 3 EQUAL PIECES DOWEL ②

DRILL, INSERT DOWELS AND GLUE 3 PIECES TOGETHER

⑥ DRILL 3 HOLES FOR WOOD SCREWS TO PREVENT SPLITTING
SAW OUT 90° GROOVE FROM 1½" DIAM.; 9" LONG PINE OR BIRCH SAPLING FOR EACH UPRIGHT POST

GROOVE OF UPRIGHT IS RIGHT ANGLE TO GROOVE OF BASE BOARD

18"

BOTTOM VIEW OF UPRIGHT

All wood used for this aquarium should be well seasoned, to prevent warping. Allow green wood several months to dry in open air, or bake for a few days in a warm oven. Follow all dimensions carefully to obtain a good fit.

Step-by-step instructions for building a sturdy, rustic aquarium are given on this and the opposite page. The only lumber needed is the hardwood board shown above; the frame itself is made from straight pine or birch saplings 1½" in diameter. Dimensions given here are for a 12-gallon capacity aquarium, but a larger or smaller size can be made from this design to meet your requirements. Right-angled grooves in corner posts are most easily cut on circular saw. Drill holes first for all screws, countersinking screw heads. Careful fitting is necessary to get the frame pieces to fit snugly against the glass.

CUT TWO SIDE RUNNERS
⑨ CUT 4 UPRIGHTS ⑤
NOTCH IS ½ WIDTH OF RUNNER
NOTCH
36"
⑧ CUT TWO END RUNNERS – THESE ARE NOT NOTCHED
9"
NOTCHES
12"

③ BASE BOARD
3 PIECES GLUED AND DOWELED TOGETHER
④ BEVEL EDGES OF BASE WITH PLANE
CUT ½" x ½" GROOVE WITH CIRCULAR SAW OR CHISEL
1"
CROSS SECTION

36"
⑦ NOTCH UPRIGHTS FOR END RUNNERS
GROOVE FOR GLASS
18"
2½" SCREWS

Ends of all cross-pieces extend 3" beyond aquarium glass. Side cross-pieces are level with aquarium top; end pieces are about 1" lower. All rest on the notched corner uprights.

by J. L. EVANS

END RUNNER
⑩ NOTCH SIDE RUNNER TO MAKE SNUG FIT THEN DRILL HOLES FOR ASSEMBLY SCREWS
SIDE RUNNER
SIDE RUNNER
END RUNNER
UPRIGHT
UPRIGHT

RUSTIC in appearance, this home aquarium filled with tiny fish, with chalky snails and clams, and with vivid green underwater plants creates a spot of interest in any home. Build one now as a place for those little creatures you have admired so much at nearby lakes and pools—watch these small fish and animals grow to maturity before your eyes, all through the summer, fall and winter.

The aquarium itself is simple to build and not at all expensive. The pieces of auto window glass, some hard wood, and the screws needed can be picked up for a few cents; the wooden framework can be cut on your vaca-

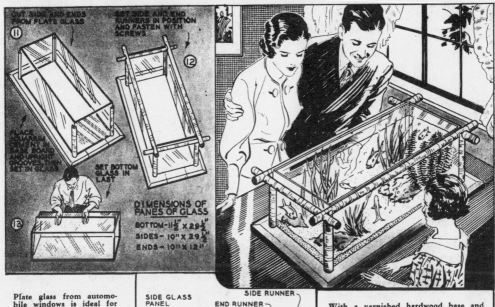

CUT SIDE AND ENDS FROM PLATE GLASS

SET SIDE AND END RUNNERS IN POSITION AND FASTEN WITH SCREWS

PLACE AQUARIUM CEMENT IN BASE BOARD AND UPRIGHT GROOVES THEN SET IN GLASS

SET BOTTOM GLASS IN LAST

DIMENSIONS OF PANES OF GLASS

BOTTOM—11½" x 29½"
SIDES—10" x 29½"
ENDS—10" x 12½"

SIDE GLASS PANEL

SIDE RUNNER
END RUNNER
UPRIGHT

SPREAD AQUARIUM CEMENT AROUND BOTTOM INSIDE EDGES—THEN SET IN BOTTOM GLASS

FORCE CEMENT INTO CRACKS

COUNTER-SUNK SCREWS

FELT

Plate glass from automobile windows is ideal for an aquarium. Straight cuts are necessary, especially at the corners where a watertight joint is required. Aquarium cement will fill up the smaller cracks. Bottom glass is set in last. Cut all pieces to dimensions given, set up on baseboard, trace around inside and outside edges, then cut the ¼" deep grooves into which glass will fit, using a chisel or circular saw for routing.

With a varnished hardwood base and rustic paper birch frame pieces, the completed aquarium makes an attractive piece of furniture for any home. To avoid excessive growth of your water plants, place the aquarium where sunlight will strike it directly for only an hour or so each day. Light coming from above, as in nature, is the best.

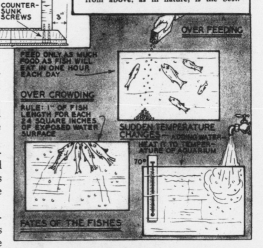

OVER FEEDING

FEED ONLY AS MUCH FOOD AS FISH WILL EAT IN ONE HOUR EACH DAY

OVER CROWDING

RULE: 1" OF FISH LENGTH FOR EACH 24 SQUARE INCHES OF EXPOSED WATER SURFACE

SUDDEN TEMPERATURE CHANGES — ADDING WATER, HEAT IT TO TEMPERATURE OF AQUARIUM

FATES OF THE FISHES

tion trip, if there are no suitable trees near your home. By following carefully the instructions given in the sketches for the construction of such an aquarium, you should have no difficulty in providing exactly the right living conditions for its inhabitants.

Aquarium cement is used to make watertight joints between the panes of glass and between the glass and the baseboard. This may be obtained at any pet shop, or may be made up at home.

Spread cement into the grooves in the baseboard, using only enough to fill the cracks when the glass is set in. Now assemble the aquarium piece by piece, applying cement to each joint and to the insides of the corner posts. Block up the glass from the inside to keep it in position until the cement hardens.

You still have one pane of glass left—this is to go on the bottom of the aquarium, and

MAKING AQUARIUM CEMENT

Mix together 1 part white sand, 1 part plaster of Paris, 1 part litharge, and ⅓ part powdered resin, then add linseed oil and clear varnish slowly, carefully working in each small portion of oil. Add just enough oil, after the lumpy stage is reached, to make a stiff, smooth, and thick paste. This formula is recommended for its strength, permanence, and harmlessness to the aquarium inhabitants.

should fit in snugly. Place a layer of aquarium cement all around the inside edges of the baseboard and on the ends of the glass pane being set in. Now allow the tank at least 48 hours to dry.

When the aquarium has been cleaned and washed, place in a 2″ layer of sand or gravel.

Pour water into the aquarium to a depth of about six inches, then put in the plants, pressing their roots firmly into place.

Plants which generally give best results in a home aquarium are *Vallisneria* (eelgrass) and *Elodea* (water weed). Various other plants found in ponds and slow streams may also be used.

In stocking the aquarium use only those animals which live in quiet pools and lakes, not in running water. Sticklebacks, mud minnows, and shiners are good ones with which to start.

About a dozen small snails may be kept in the tank. Snails are valuable as scavengers, and also keep the glass free of the green algae.

Clams should be small, and there should not be more than one per gallon of water.

The snails and clams will provide their own food, as they live mostly upon plants. Most of the other occupants may be fed small amounts of finely chopped raw meat, or small insects; raw beef is taken readily by fish.

Rustic Window Boxes

Instead of using an ordinary green-painted window box, why not make an artistic one in which the color does not clash with the plants contained in it but rather harmonizes with them.

Such a window box can be made by anyone having usual mechanical ability, and will furnish more opportunities for artistic and original design than many other articles of more complicated construction.

The box proper should be made a little shorter than the length of the window to allow for the extra space taken up in trimming and should be nearly equal in width to the sill, as shown in Fig. 1. If the sill is inclined, as is usually the case, the box will require

a greater height in front, to make it set level, as shown in Fig. 2.

The box should be well nailed or screwed together and should then be painted all over to make it more durable. A number of ½-in. holes should be drilled in the bottom, to allow the excess water to run out and thus prevent rotting of the plants and box.

Having completed the bare box, it may be trimmed to suit the fancy of the maker. The design shown in Fig. 1 is very simple and easy to construct, but may be replaced with a panel or other design. One form of panel design is shown in Fig. 3.

Trimming having too rough a surface will be found unsuitable for this work as it is difficult to fasten and cannot be split as well as smooth trimming. It should be cut the proper length before being split and should be fastened with brads. The half-round hoops of barrels will be found very useful in trimming, especially for filling-in purposes, and by using them the operation of splitting is avoided. After the box is trimmed, the rustic work should be varnished, in order to thoroughly preserve it, as well as improve its appearance.

Fig. 2

Fig. 1

Fig. 3

Artistic Flower Boxes

THE rustic beauty of natural bark is the novel feature of this turned lamp. Just enough turning is done to finish the ends of the base log and the pedestal.

Cottonwood, which is also often called poplar, is used because it is a tough, close-grained white wood that does not crack, and the bark does not come off when dried. The logs, however, must be cured out of doors for a year before the wood can be used.

Cottonwood seedlings can be found along almost any river or stream and they often grow beside country roads. They should be cut and stood up in the back yard for use next year. Four or five of these logs from 2 to 4 in. in diameter will provide material for several lamps and other small articles. The lamp illustrated is about a two-hour project.

A piece of log 11 in. long and 3 in. in diameter is used for the pedestal. This is turned as shown at B in the drawing, leaving a 4½-in. section of bark as shown. A ¼-in. hole is bored from each end through the center of the pedestal for the lamp cord.

The cottonwood logs should be cured out of doors for about a year before using. The lamp itself can be made in two hours

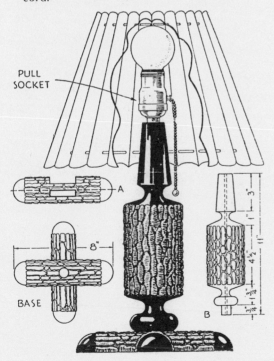

PULL SOCKET

A

8"

BASE

3"
1"
11"
4½"
¾" 1¾"

B

The base log is 8 in. long and 2 in. in diameter. The ends are turned round, and the log is sawed in two as indicated by the dotted line A. The halves of the base log are then notched and fitted together at right angles. The tenon at the bottom of the pedestal is fitted into the ¾-in. hole bored in the center of the base.

The turned parts are stained and varnished, and when this finish has dried, the entire lamp, bark and all, is given two coats of varnish. A pull socket is mounted at the top by means of a ⅛-in. pipe nipple. A 12-in. shade is the right size to use, and it must be the bulb-gripping type. The shade should be autumn colored and preferably fluted to harmonize with the log motif. Many commercial shades of this type are available.—HAROLD JACKSON.

Electric Fixtures
Made from SAPLINGS

HARMONIZE WITH ANY RUSTIC SETTING

By Leonard F. Merrill

A PAIR of electric wall fixtures or sconces made from saplings are decorative additions to any rustic-finished attic or basement room or to a cabin or summer cottage.

Materials. The following may be purchased at any store carrying electrical fixtures: 2 candle converters for adapting candlesticks to hold electric candle lights; 2 candle-fixture sockets; 2 candle covers; 2 flame bulbs; 1 plug cap; and about 12 ft. of silk-covered, parallel wire lamp cord. The rustic part of the sconces must come from the woods—two saplings about 1½ in. in diameter, with a bend as shown. A shield or back plate may be used or not, as desired. If used, two boards about 6 by 10 in. will be needed.

Tools. A saw, screw driver, knife, ¼-in. bit, another bit (about ¾-in.) to make a tight-fitting hole for the converter, a brace, and a pair of pliers will be all you need.

Saplings. Take a hatchet or saw and go out into the nearest woods where you find no restrictions or where you have received permission to cut two saplings. Almost any kind of wood will do if it is solid wood and not pithy at the heart. Birch, maple, beech, and hickory are all good.

Look for a sapling about 1½ in. in diameter that has a bend similar

to the one shown. These bends may be found at various locations in the sapling, but one place in particular is near the base where it started to grow up straight, then for some reason changed its mind and twisted out of plumb, but later on grew up again in a vertical position. Another location for this bend is where two branches have started, but one of them has failed to flourish, the other continuing to grow very nearly as large as it was before the branching started.

One of the wall fixtures, the bracket of which is made from a crooked piece cut from a sapling. The lights are best used in pairs as at the left

The shield, if one is used, is fastened to the brackets with screws. Note the groove in which the parallel wire lamp cord goes before shield is hung

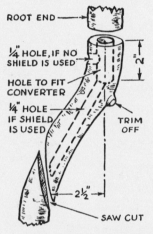

ROOT END

¼" HOLE, IF NO SHIELD IS USED

HOLE TO FIT CONVERTER

¼" HOLE IF SHIELD IS USED

TRIM OFF

2"

2½"

SAW CUT

How the sapling is cut. When a shield is used, a long ¼-in. hole must be bored; otherwise a short one will be sufficient

Construction. The lower end of the bent sapling is to be the upper end of the finished sconce, so reverse the natural position of the wood. With the sapling in the new position, saw off the top end at right angles to the vertical axis, about 2 in. above the bends.

The other end is sawed at right angles to the first cut or parallel to the vertical axis. There should be about 2½ in. clearance between this second cut and the center of the first end cut. Cut the second sapling the same as the first to make a matched pair as uniform as possible.

In the center of the upright end, bore a hole that will make a tight fit for the converter and a little deeper than the converter is long.

A ¼-in. hole for the wire is now bored in each piece. If a shield is to be used, a hole will have to be bored up through the full length of the piece, intersecting the larger hole at its base. Another hole will have to be bored through the shield piece to meet the hole in the lower end of the sconce piece. Where no shield is used, the ¼-in. hole is bored from the back of the upright piece near the top, intersecting the larger hole at a point that will come opposite the small hole in the converter.

Fasten the sconce piece to the shield with two screws, being careful not to drive them through the holes bored for the wires.

Wiring. Thread the wire through the holes in the sconce and then through the converter. Force the converter into place in the sconce. Screw the socket into place on the converter and attach the ends of the wire. Place the insulator on and slip the candle cover in place.

Measure the space between the points where you plan to have the sconces and cut the wire about 1 ft. longer than this. It may be possible to hide the wire behind a molding, mantel, or some other part of the room construction. This should be decided before cutting the wire so as to allow for it in measuring. Wire the second sconce as you did the first with the exception of cutting the wire.

Fasten the finished fixtures to the wall with screws. Splice the wire from the first sconce to the wire from the second, and insulate the joints with both rubber and friction tape.

Attach the plug cap to the end of the wire, screw the bulbs into place, and plug into the nearest outlet.

OLD TIME PLANS DISCOVERED

Grandfather's Secrets Revealed!

As result of countless hours of research we have re-discovered a wealth of useful ideas, plans and projects. Originally published in the "good old days" of our granddaddys, we've compiled these plans into a series of how to plan books for todays craftsmen. Each "idea book" is packed with instructions and plans plus measured drawings of each project.

HOW TO MAKE. . .

ACTION TOYS

OUTDOOR FURNITURE

WEATHERVANES
and
WHIRLIGIGS

COLONIAL FURNITURE

MISSION FURNITURE

FENCES
and
TRELLIS'S

MISSION STYLE
LAMPS

MISSION STYLE
METAL WORKS PROJECTS

GAMES
&
PUZZLES

SNOWSHOES

GYMNASIUM and
SPORTS EQUIPMENT

CANOES

SEND FOR OUR FREE LIST

SMITH BROOK PRESS
RR 1 Box 217D
Diamond Point, NY 12824